Leadership, Organizational Change and Sensemaking

Organizational change literature often focuses on the leaders role in giving sense to others of the need for change, and there is a plethora of models and recipes on how to influence employees thinking about change, organizational design and performance. Notwithstanding this ready supply of advice, research has shown that up to 90% of change programs fail to deliver their expected outcomes. One of the reasons for this which has been neglected in the literature is that successful change in thinking starts with how leaders first make sense of the need for change and the challenges this poses to their own thinking.

This book surfaces the elements behind leader sensemaking that add to or detract from their ability to critically question their current thinking. Leaders and interventionists have lacked practical and pragmatic advice on how to influence the process. This book is the culmination of 10 years of research spent working with leaders in organizations as they interpreted the need for change and made choices about engaging, or not, with transformational change methodologies. It reveals nine elements of sensemaking displayed by organizational leaders as they grapple with challenges to their current orthodoxies about how to lead and organize in times of change.

The book shows the latest state of knowledge on the topic and will be of interest to researchers, academics, practitioners and students in the fields of leadership, change and organizational development.

Dr Ronald Skea is a Business Agility Senior Manager at Lloyds Banking Group and a Chartered Fellow of the Chartered Institute of Personnel and Development and a Fellow of the Chartered Management Institute, UK.

Routledge Studies in Organizational Change & Development

Series Editor: Bernard Burnes

Academic Practitioner Research Partnerships
Developments, Complexities and Opportunities
Edited by Jean Bartunek and Jane McKenzie

The Social Psychology of Change Management
Theories and an Evidence-Based Perspective on Social and Organizational Beings
Steven ten Have, John Rijsman, Wouter ten Have and Joris Westhof

Organization Development and Society
Theory and Practice of Organization Development Consulting
Baruch Shimoni

Reshaping Change: A Processual Perspective, 2nd Edition
Patrick Dawson

Changing Change Management: Strategy, Power and Resistance
Darren McCabe

Leadership and Digital Change
The Digitalization Paradox
Einar Iveroth and Jacob Hallencreutz

Critical Perspectives on Diversity in Organizations
Thomas Calvard

Leadership, Organizational Change and Sensemaking
Ronald Skea

For more information about this series, please visit: https://www.routledge.com/Routledge-Studies-in-Organizational-Change--Development/book-series/SE0690

Leadership, Organizational Change and Sensemaking

Dr Ronald Skea

Routledge
Taylor & Francis Group
NEW YORK AND LONDON

First published 2021
by Routledge
605 Third Avenue, New York, NY 10158

and by Routledge
2 Park Square, Milton Park, Abingdon, Oxon, OX14 4RN

Routledge is an imprint of the Taylor & Francis Group, an informa business

Library of Congress Cataloging-in-Publication Data
Names: Skea, Ronald, 1957- author.
Title: Leadership, organizational change and sensemaking / Dr. Ronald Skea. Description: 1 Edition. | New York : Routledge, 2021. |
Series: Routledge studies in organizational change & development | Includes bibliographical references and index.
Identifiers: LCCN 2020055969 (print) | LCCN 2020055970 (ebook) | ISBN 9780367898762 (hardback) | ISBN 9781003022503 (ebook)
Subjects: LCSH: Leadership. | Employee motivation. | Organizational change.
Classification: LCC HD57.7 .S5634 2021 (print) | LCC HD57.7 (ebook) | DDC 658.4/092--dc23
LC record available at https://lccn.loc.gov/2020055969
LC ebook record available at https://lccn.loc.gov/2020055970

ISBN: 978-0-367-89876-2 (hbk)
ISBN: 978-1-032-01475-3 (pbk)
ISBN: 978-1-003-02250-3 (ebk)

Typeset in Sabon
by MPS Limited, Dehradun

This book is for Azmi Basir without whom my research would never have started or been completed and without whom the book would have remained just an idea. Some people inspire more than they can ever know and Azmi is one of these people. Thank you Azmi.

Contents

Introduction

Why This Book?

A leader once described me as an 'organisational heretic who in times gone by would have been burned at the stake', but he meant this as a compliment. He had come to realize that transformation was not about process, it was about challenging prevailing thinking and beliefs about organizational reality and that any such challenge is frequently sensed as heresy.

I had not always been a heretic. My story followed a familiar leadership pattern to most of my contemporaries. It included a combination of experience gained from working with other leaders, attending training courses on managing change, learning from reading popular texts on organizational change, and undertaking formal management qualifications. I had spent many years building up my knowledge of the process of change management and so I couldn't understand why so many change initiatives seemed so unsuccessful at delivering the new leadership thinking and behaviours that were promised. Maybe I had read the wrong books.

Well at the time of writing this manuscript a search on the Amazon website for books with 'change and leadership' in the title produced a list of over 10,000 book titles so maybe I just needed to read a few more. This does not include an equally large volume of academic articles and journals dedicated to the topic. It might seem that there can't be much more to say and the answer to my question must be out there somewhere. An alternative view might be why, given this enormous range of books and articles, is change still such a challenge to organizations and leaders? In line with the experience of many other leaders I found the models wanting. Things never seemed to work out as they should and other people would often react negatively (i.e. resist) the approaches and tools that the change models insisted would deliver successful change. Why, I wondered, do leaders resist change?

But my research led me to understand that I had made the wrong interpretation and thus was asking the wrong question. Leaders don't resist change, they resist what they consider to be bad ideas, especially heretical ideas that challenge their own long held beliefs and ideas. The question therefore is not why leaders resist change, the question is what influences the way in which leaders make sense of change when they encounter it?

If leaders intend embarking on profound and radical change, one might reasonably assume that they are prepared for a considerable shift in their thinking about what constitutes effective leadership and organization. But comments made to me by leaders I have worked with over the years suggest that not everyone believes that leaders fully embrace transformation:

> "Everyone's a 'transformation' leader these days. They keep doing the same thing of course but they kid themselves that somehow it's transformation" (Mike - Finance Director)

> "It's not even old wine in a new bottle. It's just a different label slapped over the old label" (Sharon - Operations Director)

> "This is our ninth transformation in 10 years – good luck with making this one stick!" (Donald - Finance Director)

These leaders are implying that 'transformation' is something of a contranym in organizational settings. They felt that public-facing communications uses the language of radical change, but internally the reality may be more of the same. When Mike says 'they kid themselves' he seems to be saying that other leaders' espoused theory is at odds with their theory in action (Argyris 2004) and perhaps they are unaware of this themselves. It was this cynicism and my own experience of working with leaders who, from my perspective, resisted challenges to their current thinking that triggered my interest in better understanding how leaders make sense of deciding whether or not to engage with transformational change initiatives and what factors promoted and inhibited their decision to engage.

This book is the result of my 10 years of research using a qualitative, ethnographic active participant methodology with leaders in a variety of organizations who were seeking to initiate transformational change. In the book I identify nine elements of leader sensemaking which any interventionist or individual seeking to challenge their current thinking will need to be aware of and respond to. It is a handbook for heretics.

Summary of contents

Part 1 outlines the concepts of leading, organising and sensemaking.

Chapters 1 and 2 summarise and give context to the concepts of leadership, organizational change and sensemaking. I explore how one can observe and interpret something so cognitive and deeply personal as sensemaking.

In Chapter 3 I set the context of sensemaking in organizations by presenting the key elements of the sensemaking stories of leaders from a range of organizations whom I interviewed prior to commencing my action centred research.

Part 2 explores the elements of leaders sensemaking which I observed in the research organizations in which I worked over a period of ten years.

In Chapters 4 to 12 I introduce each of the nine elements of sensemaking. I demonstrate the influence each element had in both helping and hindering leaders embrace a change of thinking and how individuals or interventionists might cope with the elements when engaging with leaders.

Part 3 revisits post-engagement sensemaking stories of leaders.

In Chapter 13 I describe a fascinating meeting of global leaders from a large organization I was working with and which was specifically set up to allow a collective 'making sense' of their experiences during and immediately after engaging with a transformational change intervention. I will demonstrate how sensemaking is a dynamic and iterative process in which history is often collectively deconstructed and reconstructed in order to make for a better story.

Part 4 pulls together the findings of my research.

The final chapter pulls together the research findings and explains why rather than focussing on how to 'manage' change interventionists and leaders would be better starting with an understanding of sensemaking of change. There is no step-by-step guide or 'do this and get that' recipe for individual leaders or interventionists. Instead there is an understanding of the complexity and unpredictability of sensemaking which although it cannot be managed nevertheless can be influenced.

Summary of Conclusions

Nine key elements of sensemaking are identified and used to understand the sensemaking process of leaders. I identify the relationship between the elements and the impact they can have in both promoting and inhibiting mindset change. I don't claim this to be an exhaustive list, but they are my interpretation of the elements at play as I observed leader sensemaking of transformational change initiatives over a 10-year period.

My research finds that the sensemaking elements are inter-related and each influences, and is influenced by, the others. My research explores the relationship between the sensemaking elements in practice in a range of organizational settings. In so doing it provides insights for leaders seeking self-development and for interventionists wishing to help others make sense of change. The book illustrates how the elements can be influenced to help create conditions for leaders to engage in reflexive practice in which they challenge their current mindsets. The book also demonstrates why changing leader mindsets is not something that has easy 'how to' recipes or that can be achieved by following simplistic step-by-step models that are prevalent in the current literature with which many practitioners are familiar.

Some of the elements I identify are existing concepts, but the disparate research has led to them being discussed as stand-alone constructs which obscures their important collective role in sensemaking. My research has synthesised a holistic understanding of these existing and new concepts and placed them into the context of leader sensemaking of organizational change.

Reference

Argyris, C. 2004. *Reasons and Rationalizations: The Limits to Organizational Knowledge*, Oxford, Oxford University Press.

Part I

Leadership, Organizational Change and Sensemaking Introduced

This book does not set out to become an encyclopedia of the enormous range of literature on leading organizational change. But if we are going to understand how leaders make sense of change we do need an overview of the literature which is likely to have influenced the current thinking of leaders prior to their engaging with change initiatives. The three chapters in Part One set the context for my research by examining the topics of leadership, change and sensemaking and then giving some practical examples of how these came together in interviews I conducted with leaders prior to engaging in my research.

1 What Are Leadership and Organizational Change?

Leadership

There is a wide field of literature on the nature and styles of leadership although most of it is focused on the implications for the role of leaders as sense*givers* in organizations rather than how they themselves make sense of change before adopting their sensegiving role. This wide variety of literature on the topic of leadership does mean, as Northouse (2013; p.2) puts it, that 'there are almost as many different definitions of leadership as there are people who have tried to define it.' Nevertheless, definitions of leadership can be broadly categorized as based on assumptions about traits, behaviors, situations and process.

Leadership Traits

It was in the second half of the 20th Century that the concept of leadership really took hold in popular business books, journals and articles. Much of the early research was on leadership traits i.e. inherent characteristics that people hold and which are good predictors of success in leadership roles. Writers produced an ever expanding and at times contradictory list of traits they argued were predictors of leadership success (Bird, 1940, Shaw, 1976, Stewart, 1963, Stogdill, 1974). Peters and Waterman (1982) re-invigorated the trait approach to leadership and other writers (Judge et al., 2004, Lord et al., 1986) continued to identify traits associated with leadership although there remained a lack of evidence that any correlation between traits and leadership was causal rather than correlational.

The trait approach has been criticized for being over simplistic and for failing to take account of situational and environmental factors that can influence the development of successful leaders. Bolden (2004) argues that despite extensive research no definitive list of traits of superior leadership performance has been established, and research by Zhang et al. (2009) has shown that situational factors play a much greater role in successful leader behaviors than any identifiable genetic factors. This failure to establish a causal link between leadership traits and successful leadership performance led writers to explore what it is successful leaders do, rather than what they are, by studying leadership behaviors.

Behavioral Leadership

Research into leader behaviors was studied by McGregor (1960) who argued that the assumptions made by leaders about employees in organizations drives their leadership behaviors and the subsequent behaviors of employees. Theory X leaders hold a fairly negative view of human nature, believing that the average employee dislikes work and will avoid it if possible. Leaders holding this view, believe that coercion and control is necessary to ensure that people work productively. However, employees treated this way will resent the coercion and control and so behave in a way that confirms the leaders view of them. It thus becomes a self-fulfilling hypothesis of employee behavior. Theory Y leaders, on the other hand, believe that the average employee wants to work, wants to do a good job and given the right leadership support will seek responsibility and autonomy. Such leaders will seek to enhance their employees' capacity to exercise a high level of imagination, ingenuity, and creativity in the solution of organizational problems. McGregor claims leaders holding different assumptions will demonstrate different approaches to leadership: Theory X leaders preferring an autocratic style and Theory Y leaders preferring a participative style.

The concept of leadership styles was further developed by Blake and Mouton (1964) who developed a Managerial Grid which focuses on task (production) and employee (people) orientations of leaders, as well as combinations between the two extremes. Their grid has concern for production on the horizontal axis and concern for people on the vertical axis and plots five basic management/leadership styles. Blake and Mouton propose that 'Team Management'—a high concern for both employees and production—is the most effective type of leadership behavior.

Likert (1967) developed the 'four systems' typology of leadership style (exploitative authoritative, consultative leadership, benevolent authoritative, and participative leadership). This typology extends the dichotomy between task and relationship orientation to consider the degree of employee involvement in decision-making and the nature of communication with the leader. Likert creates a distinction between autocratic (task-oriented) and democratic (relationship-oriented) leadership.

However, as with traits theory, critics argue that there is insufficient evidence that behavioral leadership theories are any better predictors of leadership success than trait theories and that they fail to take account of situational factors which means that 'most researchers today conclude that no one leadership style is right for every manager under all circumstances (Bolden, 2004, p.10).

Situational/Contingency Leadership

Other writers have sought to understand these situational and environmental influences on leadership and the resulting contingency theories consider both individual and situational factors together in determining leader effectiveness. Fiedler (1964, 1967) argues that there is no single best way to lead; instead the leaders' style should be selected according to the situation. His approach distinguishes between leaders who are task or relationship oriented. Task oriented leaders focus on the task in hand and tend to do better in situations that have good leader-member relationships, structured tasks, and either weak or strong position power. They also do well when the task is unstructured but position power is strong, and also when the leader member relations are moderate to poor and the task is unstructured. Task oriented leaders tend to display a more directive leadership style. Relationship oriented leaders do better in all other situations and exhibit a more participative style of leadership.

Hersey and Blanchard (1977, 1988, Hersey et al., 2001) adopted a similar approach but build it around the development needs of employees at any given time. They also reject the either/or approach of task *or* relationship leadership styles by suggesting that a leader can be both task *and* relationship focused by adapting their style to the situation and needs of employees. Hersey and Blanchard argue that as the skill and maturity level of employees increases, the leader will need to adapt his/her task relationship style from directing to coaching, supporting and delegating. Tannenbaum and Schmidt (1958) suggest a similar model with a continuum of leadership styles from autocratic to democratic.

Another popular situational leadership model was developed by John Adair (1973, 2003) who argued that the leader must balance the needs of the task, team and individual. An effective leader carries out the functions and behaviors depicted by the three circles, varying the level of attention paid to each according to the situation.

Critics argue that whilst situational theories have explanatory power that helps understanding about what makes a leader effective, they are difficult to apply in practice (e.g. when attempting to change leadership behavior). As a result, researchers have tended to move on to developing new leadership theories which focus on leadership in a turbulent organizational environment.

Process Theories of Leadership

A more enduring leadership theory is that of transformational leadership. Burns (1978) is credited with developing the process led concept of leadership in which he promotes the idea of transforming leadership, with its emphasis on the leaders' ability to motivate and empower his/her followers and also the moral dimension of leadership. Burns' ideas were subsequently developed from his *transforming leaders* into a stronger process ontology of *transformational leadership* by Bass (1985, 1999, Bass and Avolio, 1994). The goal of transformational leadership is:

> ... to 'transform' people and organisations in a literal sense – to change them in mind and heart; enlarge vision, insight, and understanding; clarify purposes; make behaviour congruent with beliefs, principles, or values; and bring about changes that are permanent, self-perpetuating, and momentum building".
>
> (Bass and Avolio, 1994)

The focus of transformational leadership is on the need to understand leadership within the context of a business environment characterized by continuous disruption, crisis and change. It is claimed that transformational leadership is better able to account for the leader's ability to cope with radical change and manage the turnaround of under-performing organizations. This is supported by a growing body of research which gives empirical support for positive associations between transformational leadership and leader effectiveness (Judge et al., 2004, Judge and Piccolo, 2004, Lowe et al., 1996).

Sensemaking (see Chapter 2) is a social process and the leaders in my research were observed as they interacted with other leaders, stakeholders and staff during 'transformational' change interventions. My research and findings therefore adopted a process ontology of transformational leadership when trying to understand leader sensemaking of a postmodern influenced mindset change methodology. It involved a process view of leadership which seeks to understand the extent to which leadership is an undetermined outcome of organizational processes as opposed to being the agent of those processes. My research looks at how the sensemaking stories of leaders are framed through these organizational social processes. As Wood puts it:

> ... normative studies recognise the objective value of leadership as an intervening process between background context and later change, while treating the individual leader as a 'black box' between input and output factors. In order to open this objectivity up to conjecture, leadership research must begin to spotlight these concealed black boxes and examine the other socio-political 'actors' and their collective role in shaping a particular leadership phenomenon.
>
> (Wood, 2005; p.23)

Notwithstanding that the definitions and aspects of leader and leadership are wide, for the purpose of my research I defined leaders as decision makers whose job roles and position in the organization gave them significant influence over the structure and strategy of the organization. They sat on the Boards or Executive Teams of the respective organizations. They were the people who had collective authority to determine and implement changes to strategy. This includes people in the organization who did not have formal or structural leadership authority but whose informal influence indicated that they were key players in the leadership sensemaking that I was observing. They included internal organizational development specialists and professionals with expertise who were brought into the leadership decision-making forums. As an active participant researcher, I include myself in this definition of leadership. As a leadership coach I had no direct reports or control of any particular business function, but I exerted considerable influence over the individual and collective leadership decisions of the research organizations.

Addressing the issue of leadership in the literature is one essential element of my research, but another is the issue of change and what it means in an organizational setting. Collins (1998) argues that any study of change, if it is 'to be of any significance, practically and theoretically, should offer an analytical framework which can offer key insights into the problems and issues of contention in planning and managing change' (p.128).

It is worth noting, however, that 'change' is a polysemantic word that not only has multiple meanings but also ambiguity regarding what part of speech it forms in a given context. It can be used as a noun (change as a thing or event) or it can be a verb (change as an action or activity). From my own experience this is particularly an issue for practitioners who are comfortable using the term 'change' in many different settings and with many different, and even conflicting, meanings. Burnes (2004) captures one reason for this ambiguity when he explains that there are two issues that need to be understood—*approaches* to change and the *nature* of change.

Approaches to Change

The lack of recognition of ambiguity of the term 'change' is prevalent in many writings on organizational change in both the academic and business press. Abraham et al. (1999) point out that most change authors focus on the role of managers as leaders of change and how they implement it, i.e. the approaches to change. Collins (1998) in his study of organizational change suggests that recent research on change management has concentrated on 'the managerial role as change instigator, and manager of change' (p.2). He argues that popular business writers on change (Kanter, 1983, Kotter, 1996, Peters and Waterman, 1982, Porter, 1980, Porter, 1985) have adopted practical as opposed to theoretical accounts of change that 'tend to deploy rather limited models of work and organizations .... and have, often without realizing it, made choices and discarded competitive theoretical alternatives' (Collins, 1998, p.6).

An early and influential writer on approaches to organizational change was Lewin (1939, 1944, 1947, 1951) who developed a widely cited three-step model of change. Burnes (2004) summarizes the three steps as follows:

> *Step 1: Unfreezing.* [Lewin] ... argued that the equilibrium needs to be destabilized (unfrozen) before old behavior can be discarded (unlearnt) and new behavior successfully adopted.
>
> *Step 2:* Moving. As Schein (1996, p.62) notes, unfreezing is not an end in itself; it '... creates motivation to learn but does not necessarily control or predict the direction'.
>
> *Step 3: Refreezing.* This is the final step in the three-Step model. Refreezing seeks to stabilize the group at a new quasi-stationary equilibrium in order to ensure that the new behaviors are relatively safe from regression.

However, the planned approach to organizational change has been criticized for being 'based on the assumption that organizations act under constant conditions that can be taken into consideration and planned for' (Barnard and Stoll, 2010, p.2). Viewing organizations through a modernist lens in which they are objects of stability over time creates a concept of change as some form of external epiphenomenon disrupting this stability. This thinking is reflected in much of the Planned approach to change management which has been seen as increasingly inappropriate for modern turbulent business environments. By (2005) gives an example of this criticism when he argues that it:

> ... ignores situations where more directive approaches are required. This can be a situation of crisis, which requires major and rapid change, and does not allow scope for widespread consultation or involvement.
>
> (p.374)

Examples of such crises on a global scale were the economic shocks experienced in the 1970s and 80s, and more recently the economic crisis in 2008 and the economic shocks and recessions caused by the Covid-19 pandemic. Lewin's planned approach attracted criticism because it was seen as unable to cope with the need for rapid transformation in the face of existential challenges.

New approaches to change were developed, but the modernist thinking of organizations as solid constructs comprising rational organizational structures which are disrupted by change remained. The Culture and Excellence approach to organizations and change, was developed by writers such as Peters and Waterman (1982) and Kanter (1999, 1992, 1989). This approach argues that organizational success is dependent on organizations having a strong and appropriate culture. Strategy became the weapon for dealing with the threats of change and just as organizations are structured, so a structured approach to change was seen as being necessary. The culture needed to survive following the shocks of the economic downturn and the rise of competition from the far east in the 1970s was deemed to be one that moved away from organization based on bureaucracy to more innovative and nimble forms of structures that could adapt more readily to changing circumstances.

Although Lewin's model was criticized for being overly simplistic, Kanter et al. (1992) nevertheless acknowledge that many subsequent models of change (including her own 'Big Three' model) describe it in terms of simple step-by-step models. Schein's (1987) is another example of a modern approach developed from Lewin's three stage model. Schein's three stages are readiness for change, cognitive restructuring and refreezing. Other models which have adopted this step-by-step recipe approach to leading change include Bullock and Batten's (1985) four-stage model, Luecke's (2003) seven steps, Kotter's (1996) eight-stage process, and Kanter et al.'s (1992) ten commandments. These models of change, which have been widely embraced by organizational development practitioners, do not seem so very different from the earlier criticized planned models of change except in that they provide more steps in their prescriptions for change.

The third important approach to organizational change is the processual approach. Writers such as Pettigrew (2001), who advocate a processual approach to change, argue that it must recognize the multiple layers, timeframes and cross-organizational nature of change. In other words, change is messy and complex and the planned approach to change does not take account of this messiness and complexity. In a processual approach to change there is no equivalent to the 'refreeze' stage of Lewin's planned change model because of the recognition that organizations seldom find themselves in a stable environment. Instead change is a constant and organizations must cope with a turbulent, frequently changing environment. Drawing on authorities in this area, Burnes (2004) highlights the differences and the similarities between the culture and processual approaches to change:

> Though there are distinct differences between these newer approaches to change, not least the prescriptive focus of the Culture-Excellence approach versus the analytical orientation of the processualists, there are also some striking similarities which they claim strongly challenge the validity of the Planned approach to change. The newer approaches tend to take a holistic/contextual view of organizations and their environments; they challenge the notion of change as an ordered, rational and linear process; and there is an emphasis on change as a continuous process which is heavily influenced by culture, power and politics.
>
> (p.990)

The influence of culture, power and politics point to the importance of understanding leader sensemaking as these will undoubtedly impact the sense leaders make of challenges to the 'status quo'. My own research, and so my own sensemaking, has been heavily influenced by a process ontology of change and transformational leadership. However, as well as being clear on my approach to change, my research also needs to take account of the literature and perspectives on the nature of change itself and I now move on to this.

Nature of Change

In my own experience as a practitioner prior to undertaking my research and conducting a literature review, I tended to confuse the *approaches* to change with the *nature* of change. Writers have broadly fallen into three categories of thinking about the nature of change. The first category which was dominant until the 1970s considers change to be planned and incremental. In this way of thinking transformation is simply the point at which a cumulative series of small change comes to be recognized and categorized as large-scale transformational change. In the 1980s, two new perspectives on change emerged: the punctuated equilibrium model and the continuous transformation model.

The punctuated equilibrium model proposes that organizational change is an evolutionary process over long periods of time and that stability is the norm, but that this relative stability is occasionally punctuated with short periods of rapid change. It is evolution punctuated with occasional revolution. Rather than transformation being an interpretation or bracketing of a series of progressive small change into a perceived large change, there are actually distinct periods when organizations go through rapid and large-scale change.

Writers proposing the continuous transformational nature of change argue that the incremental and punctuated equilibrium models are flawed because they are both based on a notion of prevailing stability. Change may be gradual or sudden and disruptive but in both cases the organization returns to a stable state. The continuous transformation model is based on an assumption that change is the natural and continuous order of things. If organizations are to survive the leaders within them must recognize this reality and continuously and constantly change in response to changes in their environment. In this new reality there is never a 'stable state' because change is the new norm.

The dominance of the incremental and punctuated equilibrium thinking about change might help explain the findings of research into the effectiveness of organizational change initiatives. Balogun and Hope Hailey (2004) report a failure rate of around 70 per cent of all change programs to deliver their expected outcomes. Siegal et al. (1996) report an even more dramatic failure rate of 90 per cent of studied change programs to deliver expected outcomes. If change programs are as spectacularly unsuccessful as the above research suggests, it begs the question of why the prescriptions for change put forward by both planned and processual change approaches fail to deliver what they promise. Siegal et al. (1996) suggest that while some of the reasons for failure relate to the *content* of change programs, many of the reasons for the high failure rate are failings in the change *process*. However, by process, most writers mean the steps for implementing change, which remains seen as some sort of external and even existential threat to real, rational and stable structures called organizations. They do not question the fundamental ontology of change and it is to a discussion of that notion that I now turn.

A Postmodern Perspective on Organization and Change

Postmodern thinking might be better called pre-modern thinking since it takes the opposing side of philosophical arguments that began two and a half thousand years ago. Chia (2003) challenges the perception of change as an activity that happens to, but is separate from, an organization and argues against the 'privileging of form, being, order, stability, identity and presence over becoming, formlessness, flux, difference, deferral and change' (p.113). He presents a postmodern ontology of change which moves the debate from planned change, whether incremental, punctuated equilibrium or continuous, to one of postmodern process in which he argues that postmodern processual perspectives of change actually stem from 5th-Century BC Greek metaphysical writings of Heraclitus and Parmenides which have driven two opposing lines of thought with Heraclitus arguing for an understanding of the environment as a state of constant flux and change from which a new environment is constantly emerging, whereas Parmenides argued that reality was permanent and unchanging.

However, studies of even earlier 6th-Century BC Chinese metaphysical writings demonstrate a similar but unconnected conflict between the ideas of Daoism and Confucianism. Although postmodern organizational theory has returned to the ideas of the Laozi and Heraclitus, Confucian and Parmenidean-informed mindsets have dominated Western thought. Parmenidean ontology is reflected in the development of Scientific Management and modernist thinking on organizations as stable entities and in which change is viewed as an epiphenomenon.

This is the punctuated equilibrium model of change but in an alternative postmodern Heraclitan influenced process ontology of change the punctuated equilibrium model is reversed and instead of organization being a noun it becomes a verb:

> ... organization and order represents the cumulative productive efforts of human intervention to temporarily stave off the nomadic and immanent forces of change. Contrary to the commonly held view, order and organization do not reflect the law of things but their exception. They are the outcome of an existential 'Will to Order'.
>
> (Chia, 2003, p.134)

So rather than stable organizational entities (organization as a thing or noun) which are subjected to occasional change, change becomes a pervasive and permanent state. But the modernist will is to create organizational order to help us make sense of the chaos of existence (organization as an activity or verb) and the result has been the idea of change as some sort of epi-phenomenon which can be managed and controlled. A process ontology of the world as in constant flux may help us understand the finding by Siegal et al. (1996) that only 10% of change programs succeed in achieving their original planned outcomes. The Parmenidean ontology of change is reflected in the planned approach to change in which models and prescriptions for change assume that change is an intervention that can be planned, managed and desired outcomes achieved. The Heraclitan ontology of change reflects an emergent approach in which continuous and ongoing adaptation is necessary. Rather than managing change you are riding the tiger – you can't get off or it will consume you, you are not in control of where the tiger goes or what it does, and the best you can do is adapt to the constantly changing circumstances. From this perspective it is not in the least surprising that up to 90% of change initiatives fail to deliver their planned outcomes, the surprise is that 10% claim that they do. One cannot plan specific outcomes when the context and circumstances driving any actions will inevitably and inexorably change rendering specifics inappropriate. A process view of change in organizations emphasizes that change is continuous and that organizations must continuously adapt to their changing environment.

Similarly, the sensemaking model of Weick et al. (2005) recognizes the postmodern view of organization as always becoming and never being:

> Viewed as a significant process of organizing, sensemaking unfolds as a sequence in which people concerned with identity in the social context of other actors engage ongoing circumstances from which they extract cues and make plausible sense retrospectively, while enacting more or less order into those ongoing circumstances.
>
> (p.409)

The logic of a postmodern ontology of change as the natural and continuous state of affairs leads to an understanding that change is not something to be 'led' with deliberate interventions but rather something to be navigated and responded to appropriately. The studies that have found that most change initiatives did not achieve their planned objectives does not mean that change did not happen. Leaders can choose to do nothing and change will still sweep over them. It is the idea that change can be precisely predicted and controlled that is the failing of the planned and punctuated equilibrium change models that dominate the literature.

The idea that change cannot be 'led' in the traditional sense is a challenge to the current reality of leaders used to enacting planned or emergent change models. This postmodern challenge was one of the elements of the business methodologies used in my research and that led me to identify the nine elements of their sensemaking, and which any interventionist working with leaders or any leader seeking to develop their current thinking should understand and react to. However, before discussing each of the nine elements I will give an overview of the concept of sensemaking in Chapter 2.

References

Abraham, M., Griffin, D. & Crawford, J. 1999. Organisation change and management decision in museums. *Management Decision*, Vol. 37 No. 10, 736–751.

Adair, J. 1973. *Action-Centred Leadership*, New York, McGraw-Hill.

Adair, J. 2003. *The Inspirational Leader: How to Motivate, Encourage & Achieve Success*, London, Kogan Page.

Balogun, J. & Hope Hailey, V. 2004. *Exploring Strategic Change*, London, Prentice Hall.

Barnard, M. & Stoll, N. 2010. *Organisational Change Management: A Rapid Literature Review*, Bristol, Centre for Understanding Behaviour Change.

Bass, B. 1985. *Leadership and Performance beyond Expectations*, New York, Free Press.

Bass, B. 1999. Two decades of research and development in transformational leadership. *European Journal of Work and Organizational Psychology*, Vol. 8, 9–32.
Bass, B. M. & Avolio, B. J. 1994. *Improving Organizational Effectiveness through Transformational Leadership*, Thousand Oaks, CA, Sage Publications.
Bird, C. 1940. *Social Psychology*, New York, Appleton-Century.
Blake, R. & Mouton, J. 1964. *The Managerial Grid: The Key to Leadership Excellence*, Houston, Gulf Publishing Co.
Bolden, R. 2004. What is leadership? *Leadership South West. Research Report*, Vol. 1, 1–37.
Bullock, R. J. & Batten, D. 1985. It's just a phase we're going through: A review and synthesis of OD phase analysis. *Group and Organization Studies*, Vol. 10, 383–412.
Burnes, B. 2004. Kurt Lewin and the planned approach to change: A re-appraisal. *Journal of Management Studies*, Vol. 41, 977–1002.
Burns, J. M. 1978. *Leadership*, New York, Harper and Row.
By, R. T. 2005. Organisational change management: A critical review. *Journal of Change Management*, Vol. 5, 369–380.
Chia, R. 2003. Organization theory as a postmodern science. *In:* Tsoukas, H. & Knudsen, C. (eds.) *The Oxford Handbook of Organization Theory: Meta-Theoretical Perspectives*. (pp. 113–142). Oxford: Oxford University Press.
Collins, D. 1998. *Organizational Change: Sociological Perspectives*, London, Routledge.
Fiedler, F. E. 1964. A contingency model of leadership effectiveness. *In:* Berkowitz (ed.) *Advances in Experimental Social Psychology*. (pp. 149–190). New York: Academic Press.
Fiedler, F. E. 1967. *A Theory of Leadership Effectiveness*, New York, McGrawHill.
Hersey, P. & Blanchard, K. H. 1988. *Management of Organizational Behavior: Utilizing Human Resources*, Englewood Cliffs, Prentice Hall International.
Hersey, P. & Blanchard, K.H. 1977. *Management of Organizational Behaviour*, Englewood Cliffs, Prentice Hall.
Hersey, P., Blanchard, K. H., & Johnson, D. E. 2001. *Management of Organizational Behavior: Leading Human Resources*, New Jersey, Prentice Hall.
Judge, T. A., Colbert, A. E. & Ilies, R. 2004. Intelligence and leadership: A quantitative review and test of theoretical propositions. *Journal of Applied Psychology*, Vol. 89, 542–552.
Judge, T. A. & Piccolo, R. F. 2004. Transformational and transactional leadership: A meta-analytic test of their relative validity. *Journal of Applied Psychology*, Vol. 89, 755–768.
Kanter, R. M. 1983. *The Change Masters: Innovation & Entrepreneurship in the American Corporation*, New York, Simon & Schuster Inc.
Kanter, R. M. 1999. Managing the extended enterprise in a globally connected world. *Journal of Organizational Dynamics*, Vol. 28, 7–23.

Kanter, R. M., Stein, B. A. & Jick, T.D. 1992. *The Challenge of Organizational Change: How Companies Experience It and Leaders Guide It*, New York, The Free Press.

Kanter, R. M. 1989. *When Giants Learn to Dance: Mastering the Challenges ofStrategy,Management,and Careers in the 1990s*, London, Unwin.

Kotter, J. P. 1996. *Leading Change*, Boston, Harvard Business School Press.

Lewin, K. 1939. Field theory and experiment in social psychology: Concepts and methods. *The American Journal of Sociology*, Vol. 44, 868–896.

Lewin, K. 1944. A research approach to leadership problems. *Journal of Educational Sociology*, Vol. 17, 392–398.

Lewin, K. 1947. Frontiers in group dynamics. *Human Relations*, Vol. 1, 5–41.

Lewin, K. 1951. *Field Theory In Social Science*, New York, Harper & Brothers.

Likert, R. 1967. *The Human Organization. Its Management and Value*, New York, McGraw-Hill.

Lord, R. G., De Vader, C. L. & Alliger, G. M. 1986. A meta-analysis of the relation between personality traits and leadership perceptions: An application of validity generalization procedures. *Journal of Applied Psychology*, Vol. 71, 402–410.

Lowe, K. B., Kroeck, K. G. & Sivasubramaniam, N. 1996. Effectiveness correlates of transformation and transactional leadership: A metaanalytic review of the MLQ literature. *Leadership Quarterly*, Vol. 7, 385–425.

Luecke, R. 2003. *Managing Change and Transition*, Boston, Harvard Business School Press.

Mcgregor, D. 1960. *The Human Side of Enterprise*, New York, McGraw Hill.

Northouse, P. G. 2013. *Leadership: Theory and Practice*, Thousand Oaks, Sage.

Peters, T. & Waterman, R. 1982. *In Search of Excellence*, New York, Harper and Row.

Pettigrew, A. M. 2001. Management research after modernism. *British Journal of Management*, Vol. 12, S61–S70.

Porter, M. 1980. *Competitive Strategy: Techniques for Analysing Industries and Competitors*, London, Macmillan.

Porter, M. 1985. *Competitive Advantage: Creating and Sustaining Superior Performance*, London, Free Press.

Schein, E. H. 1987. *Process Consultation Volume 2: Lessons for Managers and Consultants*, Reading, MA., Addison-Wesley.

Schein, E. H. 1996. Three cultures of management: The key to organizational learning. *Sloan Management Review*, Vol. 39, 9.

Shaw, M. 1976. *Group Dynamics*, New York, McGraw-Hill.

Siegal, W., Church, A. H., Javitch, M., Waclawski, J., Burd, S., Bazigos, M., Yang, T., Anderson-Rudolph, K. & Warner Burke, W. 1996. Understanding the management of change: An overview of managers' perspectives and assumptions in the 1990s. *Journal of Organizational Change Management*, Vol. 9, 54–80.

Stewart, R. 1963. *The Reality of Management*, London, Pan/Heinemann Books.

Stogdill, R. M. 1974. *Handbook of Leadership: A Survey of Theory and Research*, New York, Free Press.

Tannenbaum, R. & Schmidt, W. 1958. How to choose a leadership pattern: Should a leader be democratic or autocratic - or something in between? *Harvard Business Review*, Vol. 37, 95–102.

Weick, K. E., Sutcliffe, K. M. & Obstfeld, D. 2005. Organizing and the process of sensemaking. *Organization Science*, Vol. 16, 409–421.

Wood, M. 2005. The fallacy of misplaced leadership. *Centre for Leadership Studies*. (pp. 1–34). Exeter: University of Exeter.

Zhang, Z., Ilies, R. & Arvey, R. D. 2009. Beyond genetic explanatoins for leadership: The moderating role of the social environmnet. *Organizational Behavior and Human Decision Processes*, Vol. 110, 118–128.

2 What Is Sensemaking and How Can You Observe It in Practice?

My research was underpinned by Weick's studies of organizational sensemaking (1988, 1993, 1995a, 1995b, 1999, 2000, 2001, 2002, Weick et al., 2005), Schon's work on the displacement of concepts and the reflective practitioner (Schon, 1963, 1983), cognitive dissonance (Beauvois and Joule, 1996, Festinger, 1957) and early gestalt psychology (Koffka, 1935).

Weick is a social constructivist and argues that sensemaking requires us to look for explanations and answers in terms of how people see things rather than structures or systems. Issues such as strategies, change and problems are not things that exist independently in organizations—their source is in peoples' ways of thinking. Sensemaking occurs after organizational members experience unexpected outcomes from, or some sort of break in the routine of, organizational life. It is therefore a retrospective activity which happens 'after' something has caught our attention or interest. And it is a process of making sense of that which we have just noticed. At an individual level it is 'a process in which individuals develop cognitive maps of their environment' (Ring and Rands, 1989, p.342).

It is 'making sense of uncertain situations that initially make no sense' (Weick, 1995a, p.4) and it is 'how people structure the unknown' (Waterman Jnr, 1990). Weick points out that 'how they construct what they construct, why, and with what effects are the central questions for people interested in sensemaking' (1995a, p.4). My research and this book seek to address these very questions.

Sensemaking shares much in common with a postmodern ontology of change. Weick argues 'that time exists in two forms, as pure duration and as discrete segments' (1995a, p.25). Pure duration is a constant stream of experience, a 'coming-to-be and passing-away that has no contours, no boundaries, and no differentiation' (Schultz, 1967) but which we experience as consisting of distinct events by 'stepping outside the stream of experience and directing attention to it' (Weick, 1995a, p.25).

I have observed examples of this reality construction in the various global organizations in which I have worked. Every organization operates in the continuous flow of experience, but each creates significance around certain dates in the calendar that would otherwise have no significance. The budget and accounting process is a common example of this. One of the UK organizations I worked in had a financial year aligned to the tax year which starts on 6th April each year. An otherwise unremarkable day in the calendar each year has now taken on tremendous importance and generates enormous planning and resourcing to meet the end of financial year requirements in March and planning activities for next year's budget. However, companies I worked for based in Singapore and Canada attached no significance to the 6th April whatever. This was just another day in the calendar. The reason was that their constructed reality revolved around a financial year starting on 1st January and ending on 31st December. Another example of this financially driven construct of reality was the difference between quarterly reporting of financial performance in all the companies I worked for except a Danish company which used trimester accounting periods in which significant dates were entirely different from the other companies.

Other writers on postmodern Organizational Theory have identified that this tendency for cognitive extracting and bracketing of events from the constant stream of experience has led to the modernist incremental and punctuated equilibrium views of change as an epiphenomenon. Chia (2003) argues that this carving up of flux into discrete segments is done for good reason – it helps us make sense of the messy complexity of the world we live in and 'life-experiences are then made more amenable to instrumental manipulation and control' (p.129). Seddon (2003) argues that this desire for order and control, which he calls a command and control mindset, is a feature of leadership in organizations.

The early Gestalt psychologists (not to be confused with modern Gestalt therapy) recognized the concept of pure duration and the problems that bracketing this continuous flow into discrete segments causes to our sensemaking, not least because of the difficulties inherent in the concept of time. Koffka (1935) argues that 'the idea that time could be bracketed into past, present and future is absurd as the past is no longer real, the future has not become real and "the present" is undefinable' (p.424). He uses the example of taking any interval of time and making it shorter and shorter – 'but however short we make it still remains an **interval**, it still has duration' (Koffka, 1935, p.425). A time interval can be halved and halved again infinitely without ever reaching a value of 0 but in the process any meaningful concept of 'interval' and 'time' is lost as in Zeno's paradox. In Zeno's paradox of Achilles and the tortoise, Achilles is racing the tortoise which is given a head start. After a time, Achilles will have run the head start distance bringing him to the tortoise's starting point. However, during this time, the tortoise has traveled a further distance and it will then take Achilles some additional time to run that extra distance, by which time the tortoise will have traveled a bit farther; and this whole cycle will continue. Thus, whenever Achilles reaches somewhere the tortoise has been, he still has farther to go. Therefore, because there are an infinite number of points Achilles must always reach where the tortoise has already been, he can never overtake the tortoise.

Despite this paradox people cope with the constant stream of experience by creating breaks and categorizing them as 'change'. The points at which we bracket the experience we are focusing on is when we perceive the current state of affairs to be different from how it was, and so how we expected it to be. Weick argues that people perceive this difference as a disruption to some perceived status quo and make sense of it by initially looking 'for reasons that will enable them to resume the interrupted activity and stay in action. If resumption of the project is problematic, sensemaking is biased either toward identifying substitute action or toward further deliberation' (Weick, 1995a, p.409)

In the context of Organizational Theory, Weick argues that this sensemaking activity allows leaders to understand a *perceived* change in the environment and take action as appropriate. Thus far, sensemaking could be seen as a rational and logical process that informs action. The emphasis on comprehension of events leading to a springboard for action implies a process of interpretation and rational decision-making. Once you have made sense of unexpected events then decisions on action become much clearer. However, thinking of sensemaking as rational and logical would be to misunderstand a complex and messy process and we will see later why. The first challenge I faced was how to observe and capture this messiness whilst working with leaders.

Qualitative Research

How do you 'observe' the internal cognitive processes that form the basis of an individual's sensemaking? This is not a topic that lends itself to traditional quantitative research and the answer is that these things can be best observed through longitudinal qualitative research. Weick (1995a) argues that sensemaking is never a solitary individual activity because any internal interpretation and sensemaking is contingent on other people – 'even monologues and one-way communications presume an audience' (p.40). My own research of leader sensemaking is based on observation and engagement with leaders over an extended period of time. I could not get into the mind of individual leaders and experience their inner sensemaking so any understanding on my part was necessarily a social process entailing the interaction of at least two people – the leader and myself as both a colleague and researcher. And there were many occasions where this was so, i.e. one-on-one discussions between me and an individual leader. But there were even more occasions where sensemaking was taking place in groups, meetings, team settings, and so forth. In these situations, the social nature of sensemaking became more evident, and it was the interaction, talk and discourse in these settings that created the opportunity for my own interpretation and sensemaking of what I was observing and hearing.

My research methods were therefore qualitative in nature and in which researchers are 'interested in documenting the processes by which social reality is constructed, managed, and sustained' (Holstein and Gubrium, 2005, p.483). Qualitative research involves a naturalistic, interpretive approach and qualitative researchers 'study things in their natural settings, attempting to make sense of, or interpret, phenomena in terms of the meaning people give to them' (Denzin and Lincoln, 2005, p.3). Or as Munro and Randall assert:

> ...the social constructionist approach holds that social reality cannot be understood apart from the intersubjective meanings of the social actors involved. The aim of social constructionist research is to understand how members of a social group enact their particular realities and endow them with sense and meaning.
>
> (Munro and Randall, 2007, p.889)

My role in each of the organizations which took part in my research was not to implement structural, systemic or process changes. It was to present, and seek engagement with, counter-intuitive alternatives to current thinking about leadership, organization and change. I therefore do not focus in this book on the details or particular methodology of any intervention and instead focus on the sensemaking elements I could observe. I approached the research as an active participant observer. Many research case studies use a participant observer role in which the researcher is situated within the case study organization for certain periods of time. But in my case it went further – I was an *active* participant observer. I was leading the attempt to influence leader thinking as well as observing their sensemaking of my efforts. My active participant methodology involved working with leaders to understand and apply concepts of single and double loop learning (Argyris, 1990, 2004, Argyris and Schon, 1974). 'Single-loop learning takes place within the existing paradigm, whereas double-loop learning requires a new paradigm' (Gummesson, 2000, p.20). A significant aspect of the methodologies used in the research organizations was the use of reflexive practice. Reflexivity is a process of self-questioning and challenging of the assumptions and beliefs that underpin a person's preunderstanding. Bourdieu (1990) defines it as a systematic exploring of 'unthought categories of thought that delimit the thinkable and predetermine the thought' (p.178).

Cunliffe (2004, p.407) puts it into language more familiar to organizational practitioners, describing it as 'examining critically the assumptions underlying our actions, the impact of those actions, and from a broader perspective, what passes as good management practice.'

The transformation methodologies used in the research organizations were based on an understanding that leaders *rationalize* their current behaviors, and the resulting organizational performance, to match their current thinking. This thinking and their behaviors may not seem *rational* to an observer but ensures psychological congruence for the leader (Festinger, 1957). The methodologies then sought to get leaders to commit to guided counter-intuitive behavior (Beauvois and Joule, 1996) which can result in cognitive dissonance which can in turn lead to a situation where leaders can no longer rationalize their current behaviors and so creates an opportunity for leaders to engage in reflexive practice and double loop learning that leads to a change in thinking. The use of reflexivity and my role as an active participant over a long period constituted what is known as action research, which is a concept first developed by Lewin (1939, 1944, 1947, 1951) but has more recently stemmed from the work of Argyris and Schon (1974) and Argyris (1990, 2004) and 'emphasizes the study of practice in organizational settings as a source of new understandings and improved practice' (Kemmis and Mctaggart, 2005, p.561). Argyris's concepts of espoused theories (what leaders say) and theories in practice (leader behaviors) are used as 'key points of reference for change' (Kemmis and Mctaggart, 2005, p.561). In my active participant role I discussed and used these concepts with leaders to help them make sense of a challenge to their current thinking.

Having placed my research within the context of sensemaking I now move on to what I learned about how it impacted on leaders' responses to challenges to their current thinking about organization, leadership and change. Before embarking on my longitudinal active participant ethnographic research I conducted a more traditional research exercise of interviewing leaders who had previously engaged with the methodology I was using and who declared themselves to hold new mindsets and paradigms as a result. The next chapter captures their stories of how they made sense of this transformational shift in thinking.

References

Argyris, C. 1990. *Overcoming Organizational Defenses: Facilitating Organizational Learning*, Boston, Allyn and Bacon.

Argyris, C. 2004. *Reasons and Rationalizations: The Limits to Organizational Knowledge*, Oxford, Oxford University Press.

Argyris, C. & Schon, D. A. 1974. *Theory In Practice: Increasing Personal Effectiveness*, San Fransisco, Jossey-Bass.

Beauvois, J.-L. & Joule, R.-V. 1996. *A Radical Dissonance Theory*, London, Taylor and Francis.

Bourdieu, P. 1990. *In Other Words: Essay toward a Reflexive Sociology*, Stanford, Stanford University Press.

Chia, R. 2003. Organization theory as a postmodern science. *In:* Tsoukas, H. & Knudsen, C. (eds.) *The Oxford Handbook of Organization Theory: Meta-Theoretical Perspectives*. Oxford: Oxford University Press.
Cunliffe, A. L. 2004. On becoming a critically reflexive practitioner. *Journal of Management Education*, Vol. 28, 407–426.
Denzin, N. K. & Lincoln, Y. S. (eds.) 2005. *The Sage Handbook of Qualitative Research*, London, Sage Publications.
Festinger, L. 1957. *A Theory of Cognitive Dissonance*, Stanford, Stanford University Press.
Gummesson, E. 2000. *Qualitative Methods in Management Research*, Thousand Oaks, Sage Publications.
Holstein, J. A. & Gubrium, J. F. 2005. Interpretive practice and social action. *In:* Denzin, N. K. & Lincoln, Y. S. (eds.) *The Sage Handbook of Qualitative Research*. 3rd ed. (pp. 483–506). Oakland: Sage.
Kemmis, S. & Mctaggart, R. 2005. Participatory action research. *In:* Denzin, N. K. & Lincoln, Y. S. (eds.) *The Sage Handbook of Qualitative Research* (3rd ed.). Oakland: Sage.
Koffka, K. 1935. *Principles of Gestalt Psychology*, London, Kegan Paul.
Lewin, K. 1939. Field theory and experiment in social psychology: Concepts and methods. *The American Journal of Sociology*, Vol. 44, 868–896.
Lewin, K. 1944. A research approach to leadership problems. *Journal of Educational Sociology*, Vol. 17, 392–398.
Lewin, K. 1947. Frontiers in group dynamics. *Human Relations*, Vol. 1, 5–41.
Lewin, K. 1951. *Field Theory in Social Science*, New York, Harper & Brothers.
Munro, I. & Randall, J. 2007. 'I don't know what I'm doing. How about you?': Discourse and identity in practitioners dealing with the survivors of childhood sexual abuse. *Organization*, Vol. 14, 887–907.
Ring, P. S. & Rands, G. P. 1989. Sensemaking, understanding, and committing: Emergent interpersonal transaction processes in the evolution of 3M's microgravity research program. *In:* Van De Ven, A. H., Angle, H. L. & Poole, M. S. (eds.) *Research on the Management of Innovation: The Minnesota Studies*. (pp. 337–366). New York: Ballinger.
Schon, D. A. 1963. *Displacement of Concepts*, London, Tavistock Publications.
Schon, D. A. 1983. *The Reflective Practitioner: How Professionals Think in Action*, London, Ashgate.
Schultz, A. 1967. *The Phenomenology of the Social World*, Evanston, Northwestern University Press.
Seddon, J. 2003. *Freedom from Command & Control: A Better Way to Make the Work Work*, Buckingham, Vanguard Education Ltd.
Waterman Jnr, R. H. 1990. *Adhocracy: The Power to Change*, Memphis, Whittle Direct Books.
Weick, K. E. 1988. Enacted sensemaking in crisis situations. *Journal of Management Studies*, Vol. 25, 305–317.
Weick, K. E. 1993. The collapse of sensemaking in organizations: The Mann Gulch disaster. *Administrative Science Quarterly*, Vol. 38, 628–652.
Weick, K. E. 1995a. *Sensemaking in Organizations*, London, Sage Publications.

Weick, K. E. 2000. Emergent change as a universal in organizations. *In:* Beer, M. & Nohria, N. (eds.) *Breaking the Code of Change.* (pp. 223–241). Boston: Harvard Business School Press.

Weick, K. E. 2001. Gapping the relevance bridge: Fashions meet fundamentals in management research. *British Journal of Management*, Vol. 12, S71–S75.

Weick, K. E. 2002. Puzzles in organizational learning: An exercise in disciplined Imagination. *British Journal of Management*, Vol. 13, S7–S15.

Weick, K. E., Sutcliffe, K. M. & Obstfeld, D. 2005. Organizing and the process of sensemaking. *Organization Science*, Vol. 16, 409–421.

Weick, K. E. 1995b. What theory is not, theorizing is. *Administrative Science Quarterly*, Vol. 40, 385–390.

Weick, K. E. 1999. Conclusion: Theory construction as disciplined reflexivity: Tradeoffs in the 90s. *The Academy of Management Review*, Vol. 24, 797–806.

3 Epiphanies and Crossing the Rubicon

The Drama of Moving from Old to New Realities

Before engaging in my longitudinal active participant research I had the opportunity to engage in a more traditional research methodology and carried out semi-structured interviews with 10 senior leaders from a variety of European organizations which had undergone transformational change. I asked them individually and separately to talk through how they first made sense of the need for transformational change and how this impacted their thinking about leadership and change.

I hoped that this might provide some pointers for me both as a researcher and as a practitioner in my upcoming active participant researcher role. However, I was conscious that this was a group of 'converts' who claimed to have embraced a transformation in their mindsets. Nevertheless, I felt the interviews could provide some useful pointers into sensemaking elements that I might expect to observe in my subsequent research. Eight of the ten leaders were from private sector companies with one from a public sector organization and one from a professional body. All held senior leader roles with direct responsibility for either the whole organization or for a significant business function within their organization. There were two female and eight male interviewees. Their experience operating as senior leaders varied from 7 to 26 years. As part of my ethics research I have promised that I would not identify any leader or their organizations and so none of the initials used are their real initials and I have not given details of the organizations they were working for.

The Impact of Experience on My Thinking

I started the interviews by asking the leaders to explain how they first arrived at the conclusion that they wanted to transform their organizations. None felt obliged to stick the particulars of my questions and although I had not asked them about this, all of them started by telling me about their leadership careers. In trying to make sense of why they had decided transformation was needed it seemed important to set the scene and the context for what they were about to tell me. And so they all chose to explain their leadership development, experience and thinking prior to engaging with transformation.

WR gave a descriptive story of a learning and experience journey that had been one of increasing boundedness and which was reflective of the other leaders' stories:

> I think it was that ... I'd learnt to be a leader within a cultural norm, irrespective of which organization it was. So this is what a leader does, and I'd done things to ... put ticks in boxes in terms of, OK, well I can do that, I can budget, I can plan, I can lead people, I can coach. So I could put ticks in all of those boxes around a cultural norm, and actually ... it was bounded for me. So if you think about a bounded problem and an unbounded problem, it had kind of given myself a nice neat boundary in terms of this is what a leader does, this is what a manager does, and if you can do those things then that's what you are ... and personally I think it goes right back to when you were at school. So when you're a child and your learning's pretty unbounded and you're pretty creative, that gradually over the years you're taught to think in a certain way ... and ... education is all about ... generally ... or traditional education that I went through, was about learning things, retaining that knowledge, being able to recite it, being able to demonstrate that you understood the learning that you'd had, and then go through tests or exams that kind of proved that you'd retained that understanding and that you were competent in that particular area. It was the same in management education [WR had completed an MBA].

This seems like retrospective sensemaking of WR's traditional, and modernist, leadership development. Leadership is seen a discreet activity with neat boundaries that makes it clear when you are, and are not, a leader as opposed to the much broader and less role-specific activity of leading. WR suggests that it is organizational role that determines a leader: 'if you can do those things then that's what you are'. And being able to do those things was a result of a long process of leadership socialization which started at an early age in school and continued in her management education and work experience – a process of being 'taught to think in a certain way'. At the time, this shaping of what to think seemed to be the right thing to do, the boundedness and constraints that it placed on her only became apparent later.

DJ felt similarly constrained by experience and prescribed practice. Talking about his experience of implementing organizational change he said:

> My ... experience, my thinking was running in parallel with the organizations themselves. So my thinking at the outset of the process

> [engaging with leaders to change their thinking] would be we're going to bring about massive performance improvement, as was the clients. The closer we got to completion, the goal became "deliver the plan", not making massive performance improvement. And there would be huge celebrations ... for both parties, our team and for the client organization, when they achieved the standard [a quality standard awarded by an external body]. But looking back on it, we really didn't achieve anything.

The phrase 'my experience, my thinking was running in parallel with the organization' reflects what all the leaders told me – their thinking was shaped from direct experience in organizations. But DJ's short description makes other telling points in setting up his forthcoming mindset change. Change was very much a project with specific outcomes, and, in DJ's experience, mostly failed to deliver the planned outcomes (massive performance improvement). His experience mirrors research that up to 90% of change initiatives fail to deliver their planned outcomes (Balogun and Hope Hailey, 2004, Siegal et al., 1996). However, DJ's cynicism about the effectiveness of the change projects he was leading is retrospective sensemaking. At the time, it was huge celebrations for a job well done (gain accreditation by the Standards body) and the failure to achieve the planned performance improvements was forgotten. Thus, DJ's preunderstanding at the point of engaging with his own transformation of mindset was of traditional change project management, which at that time he considered a successful method of change.

DJ's and WR's descriptions of their roles leading to their leadership experiences were common to all the interviews. While it might come as no surprise that senior leaders in organizations have extensive experience, what these descriptions seem to illustrate is the importance of previous experience in the sensemaking process. Sensemaking does not happen in isolation from current thinking which has been shaped by previous experience. In their stories of why and then how they engaged in their own mindset change it seemed crucial to first set the scene and justify why they thought and behaved the way they did before engaging with transformation. I use the word 'justify' because the leaders seemed almost embarrassed when describing how they used to think and behave as leaders in, as more than one described it, the 'old world'.

HR summed up the importance of experience in the thinking of senior leaders when she said 'I used to think I'm experienced ... I can use my previous experience for new challenges, to take advantage from what I see, what I've seen, what I did before, I'm able to transfer to a new environment'.

'What I did before, I'm able to transfer to new environment' is a particular form of preunderstanding that many leaders will bring to new situations or roles but could lead to what Argyris (1976) calls single loop learning. There is a common joke in organizations, which runs along the lines that when someone says they have 20 years' experience what they really mean is they have one year's experience repeated 20 times. This captures the concept that experience can be static (and repetitious) or dynamic (and constantly changing). It is the degree of reflexivity engaged in which determines whether experience is single loop (one year repeated) or double loop (continuous learning and change). My interpretation of HR's comment is that she is suggesting the notion that leadership is a cumulative exercise of bringing prior experience or pre-understanding to bear on current business issues confronting the leader.

However, experience is not limited to that gained in organizations. Many of the leaders had undertaken formal management qualifications. WR talked about her management education. She was encouraged to do an MBA because it was expected of leaders in her organization, but at the time she felt this continued shaping of how to think was a good thing:

> My manager recommended to do that [get an MBA]. I got on a pilot scheme and did a Certificate of Management, and then a Diploma of Management and then my MBA. So there was a bit in it for me in terms of I could learn how to be, hopefully, a better manager and more structured, *that was my thought process at the time anyway.* But certainly it then felt that that fit their cultural norm in that there was somebody there with an MBA, so some letters that kind of were recognized within that culture as something that was kind of a cultural fit for a senior managerial role. (my italics)

DP also talked about his leadership training and the impact of Blake and Mouton's (1964) Managerial Grid on this thinking and how 'I learned as a leader we must put people in one of the boxes'. DP was illustrating the degree to which formal education using common leadership or change models can constrain leader thinking when he says he had learned to put people into boxes. The 'boxes' both direct and constrain leader thinking by imposing 'either/or' continuums in which, in the Managerial Grid for example, leadership style is one *or* other of the types on two continua.

The Drama of the 'ah-ha!' Moment

Having extensively set the scene in their stories and laid out the experiences which shaped their previous thinking, the leaders then moved on to points of high drama – which for all ten involved epiphanies when their current thinking and reality is revealed to be flawed. It was these ah-ha! moments that convinced them to engage with transformation.

DJ told me a story about a conference for leaders that he had organized. He invited a speaker to talk about organizational transformation although he knew little about him. DJ's story used a fishing metaphor to build up to the ah-ha! moment:

> I suppose at that point, at the back of the room, sitting with the AV crew with my checklist I started to really pay attention when he talked about ... setting targets and how it drove the wrong behavior, and having asked the audience how they set a target, by what method ... rather sheepishly one hand went up and the person concerned said "Well I suppose you look at what you did last month or last year and you kind of wet your finger and you go either up or down and that's how you set a target". [the speaker] explained that was still an arbitrary measure and it was at that point that he really, really had me hooked. So I became fascinated by what he was saying and he started to reel me in.

Having set about reeling him in, in a short space of time the speaker created DJ's ah-ha! moment:

> I started to realize, over the course of forty-five minutes, which was the keynote address, that my thinking really was fundamentally wrong ... and I was quite prepared to, to accept that and wanted to learn more.

I asked DJ about what seemed like a rapid realization of his flawed thinking:

Me: So would you say [the speaker] was some sort of a trigger?
DJ: There was an 'ah-ha!' moment in terms of everything that I'd focused on, in terms of business planning with clients, was all about setting targets and 'SMART'[1] objectives and agreeing inspirational missions and visions and value statements ... So when [the speaker] started to talk about targets bringing about the wrong behavior and not improving performance from the customer's perspective, it made sense to me ... So I kind of had that 'ah-ha!' moment. I'd never come across anything quite like it before.

HR also had an epiphany when listening to a speaker at a different event:

> I remember in the masterclass kind of nudging my colleagues on either side ... in a state of what, I use the word elation, but in a state of kind of panic and elation at the same time ... of I can't quite believe what I'm hearing, oh my God! I've done all the wrong things. They [other participants in the masterclass] didn't seem to be getting it and I don't know why.

I asked HR what led to this insight:

> Um ... it was a new concept, but I suppose at some intuitive level it made, it made sense, yeah, it made complete sense. I just never thought about work in that way.

WR had a similar tale to tell. She had her epiphany at leadership workshop. At first she thought this was going to be an introduction to another change and performance management 'tool' that she might be able to use:

> it was another ... kind of workshop that I was going to go on to understand ... some ... probably different tools really. I went into it sort of quite open-minded, hoping to learn, hoping to get an insight into ... some kind of ... tool that would help me to do things differently and drive change

Influenced by her previous experience, this is initially what she thought she was hearing. But then her ah-ha! moment happened:

> I went along, and for about the first week I sat there and I thought this is just what I've always done really, it's about process re-engineering. But it was over that weekend I think that I went away and one of the things that I did develop as part of my MBA was I became more reflective and ... more ... theoretical in my approach. Previously I'd been very activist/pragmatist, and I think over that weekend I reflected on what the week had been ... and what the outcomes were, and basically I completely changed my thinking that weekend.

There was a remarkable consistency between all the leaders stories about this aspect of their sensemaking. Either they had attended a workshop of some sort or had a meeting with a change consultant which led to a sudden realization that their current thinking about leadership and organization was flawed. As both a fledgling researcher and an experienced practitioner I was interested in the steps that led to this realization. As a researcher I would want to look out for similar ah-ha! moments with leaders I would be working with, and as a practitioner I was interested in what factors helped contribute to this sudden change in thinking.

So I asked the leaders if they could specify what it was that had led to them recognizing that their current thinking was flawed. WR had already told me that it was a weekend of reflection on what she had heard in the workshop that convinced her:

> But one of the things that I kept coming back to was the voice of the customer. Up to that point of course I thought I was customer focused but the material on the workshop kind of challenged that view and gave lots of examples of leaders in other organizations who thought like me but then discovered that their customers actually hated them ... and I was kind of thinking 'is that what my customers think too?

RB had his ah-ha! moment during a meeting with a change consultant:

> Well I don't think I had the, the normative experience, you know, during the meeting, but [the consultant] was eloquent enough to, to be able to outline a case study of a firm that were (sic) achieving all their targets. Just like I was achieving all my targets. Yet when he looked at performance from the customer's point of view, particularly end to end times, customer service was getting worse. Then I realized that was the same for me ... really ... because I was getting so many complaints from customers ending up on my desk. So I just had an insight, I wasn't totally convinced, but just had an insight ... became curious and wanted to learn more.

RB makes two puzzling points in this description of his moment of insight. The first is that he had not had the 'normative experience'. The methodologies the leaders were being introduced to seek to change leader thinking through the use of what is called a normative experience. Leaders are first asked to describe their leadership thinking and behaviors and the organizational performance this is producing (i.e. articulate their current reality). They then engage in action research studying actual practices and performance at various work locations to listen to and observe customer interactions and workflows. This is followed by reflexive practice to identify any difference between their thinking of how things work and what they have observed during their action research. The thinking behind this exercise is that leader perceptions and the reality they observe will usually differ and often quite substantially from their current reality. If so, the methodology assumes, the cognitive dissonance created by the discrepancy between current thinking and observed practice will mean leaders are less likely to rationalize what they have observed and will be more receptive to challenges to their current mindset. The methodologies make no claims for the creation of ah-ha! moments but if they are going to happen it might be expected it would be during or immediately following reflexive practice. However, all the leaders were telling me that they had had their epiphanies before engaging in any normative experience. It seemed that a presentation was sufficient to create the trigger for a change in thinking.

The second puzzling aspect was when RB finished by saying that despite his epiphany that his thinking was flawed he wasn't 'totally' convinced at this stage but had become curious. Whilst all the leaders described some form of epiphany after hearing a presentation perhaps, like RB, they too are actually describing a moment when curiosity was aroused. Their thinking may have been challenged and they may have had an inkling that it was flawed in some way, but actually establishing a new mindset took much longer.

Oxymorons

The stories of the leaders I interviewed seemed to contain self-evident contradictions that did not seem to bother them. Most of the leaders talked about how fast their change of thinking was but then also talked about how slow a change in thinking can be. How could their sensemaking embrace the oxymoron of a slow, fast change in thinking? One possibility is that their sensemaking led them to emphasize one aspect (speed) whilst acknowledging that the opposite is also an aspect of the methodology (slowness). The leader stories so far all had the same elements – an explanation of their preunderstanding then the drama of ah-ha! moments or sudden insights that their thinking was flawed. It might seem that the story of changing leader thinking was relatively brief and simple. A good presentation seemed to be sufficient. But there is a twist in their stories.

DJ had told me that he changed his thinking after hearing a short presentation and I asked him about this:

Me: – you said that you knew by the end of [the] presentation that your thinking was flawed. What happened next?

DJ: I suppose what I need to say at this point is that at a level, at a certain level I got this, I understood this, I thought I understood this method, and it's now been just over two years since I started using it, and having worked on several interventions … I thought that I got it … But it wasn't until recently that I really understood it

So, having said he 'got it' after the 45-minute presentation, DJ was now saying it actually took him two years to fully 'get it'.

MK (English was not his first language) had a similar tale when I asked him how long it took to change his thinking following his insight at a presentation:

> Later on, I understood that it's … a window to organization. So from that point of view, it's even more interesting for me, as it's only then I understand that how wheels is [sic] working

should be changed. The organization is too rigid, too traditional, too less customer oriented, and things like that, yeah. And the approach is something that can show a new lens to the organization, but it took me more than a year to know that.

IR summed up the difference between the dramatic ah-ha! moment when leaders claim to realize that perhaps their thinking is flawed and the slower process of actually changing their thinking:

IR: I'd been doing wrong and then I began to feel lost because I lost some confidence and wasn't sure what I should be doing instead. I started off thinking this is easy ... (laughs) ... then learned that it's bloody difficult! But now, you know, I'm quite convinced of the new thinking
Me: – how long would you say it took before you were convinced?
IR: hmm ... that's tricky one ... I was convinced from the outset in one way but then when I started to behave differently I realized that it wasn't so simple and would fall back into old bad habits. I suppose it's taken me a year or so to work through the ... what would you call it ... the challenges and see for myself that it works but that doesn't mean I don't still sometimes find myself in old world thinking mode. Old habits die hard!'

What IR could have said is that 'old thinking dies hard'. From a force field analysis model perspective (Lewin, 1951), it would seem that many years of leadership education, training and experience act as a strong restraining force against new thinking and that this can last for a number of years. The term 'old world' was used by many of the leaders and I interpreted this to be a commonly understood term to mean pre-engagement thinking about leadership and organization. It seems to be shorthand for the entirety of leader preunderstanding. 'Old world' also suggests a significant break with that preunderstanding. The metaphor of old world provides a description for the lens used to view reality in their pre-engagement days.

Thus, the initial speed and ease with which a change of thinking was presented by leaders in their ah-ha! stories were actually represented by a much longer timeframe of between one and two years. It might seem contradictory that leaders can say they had ah-ha! moments when they realized their current thinking was wrong but then say that it took up to two years before they actually 'got it' in terms of the new thinking. However, it seems to me to make sense if the ah-ha! moments are actually initial curiosity, or the glimmerings or sparks of initial recognition that the 'old ways' were not necessarily appropriate, leading to a sense of unease which opens the possibility that my current thinking is 'wrong', but it takes longer to work out what 'right' thinking is.

It's Lonely Being the Hero

Although they did not know each other, the leader stories all had a similar format. They all discussed their preunderstanding and then how they encountered the transformation methodology. As discussed in the previous section, they all also talked about experiencing some form of ah-ha! moment or insight during the initial presentations that led them to realize that their current thinking was flawed. But, as they started engaging with the methodology, the journey to full understanding took much longer.

I encouraged the leaders to talk freely about what it felt like for them as they gained their initial insights and started to engage with the methodology. At this point the leader stories exhibited some of Gabriel's (2000) poetic tropes in storytelling (see Chapter 5). The first was attribution of responsibility in which the leader was positioned as the hero of the story – someone who 'got it' and who carried the responsibility of showing others the error of their thinking as demonstrated by JL:

Me: And were you able to make any connections with your own experience and organization?

JL: The only connection was that I'd been doing the wrong stuff. That my thinking, the assumptions behind what I was doing was fundamentally wrong. It was actually, it was actually elating, it was elating ... What was depressing was that I seemed to be, without putting myself on a pedestal, I seemed to be the only person out of a hundred and twenty-one that was getting it ...'

JL wasn't the only one whose story placed them in a position of enlightenment whilst surrounded by those who still didn't get it. HR described a similar experience:

HR: The problem was that I could see what was wrong with the way we were doing things ... and ... but of course everyone else was still blind to it. I was enthusiastically trying to change things and everyone else was resolutely opposing me. I felt like ... well it was really frustrating and at the time I felt like clocking a few of them but of course now I realize it wasn't their fault as such coz they didn't know any better I suppose. Some of them still don't (laughs)'.

IR told a similar tale of how he had 'got it' but found it very difficult to help other leaders to get it:

IR: ': Making change is really a difficult process, to change an organization is really a very difficult process.

Me: What is it makes it so difficult?

IR: Ha! ... if you're talking to other leaders they all say, and they do it also in job interviews they say OK, we are a company which is constantly changing, what today is good is tomorrow not good enough anymore, and everyone's saying in this job, ah I like it, changes I like, oh I like it so much. But you will soon find out that people have a job that they're comfortable in, and they don't like changes, it's always difficult for people to change ... So it's everyone, or almost everyone, is saying I like changes but if it's really coming very near to you then they are a little bit, there is always a little bit of opposition there'.

HR outlined the difficulties of helping others change their thinking using rational argument:

HR: It's difficult working with people who can't or won't understand it ... and I don't think there's any point in me sitting and explaining in a rational sense why this is the right thing to do, it comes back to the normative experience of, I can sit and debate with managers until I'm blue in the face and I'll never convince them'.

RB also talked of the isolation of knowledge amongst ignorance:

RB: It's a curse being a new world thinker when everyone else is old world. I'm not the most patient person in the world and I don't suffer fools gladly (laughs) ... but, it's weird when ... well it's sort of everyone thinks it's you that's the fool (laughs). So yeah, I got very frustrated with people who just didn't get it and ... emm ... I mean I'm used to saying what I think and arguing my case even if I'm the only one with it ... but this was different from just having a difference of opinions. This was about seeing the world differently and for a time I was the only one seeing it that way and that was much more difficult to handle. Once I'd converted a few people (laughs) I wasn't so isolated!'

WR talked about what it feels like as you develop a different mindset:

> It's a difficult thing once you start looking at the world through a new lens and everyone else is still using the old one. You see things differently... so completely differently. I mean I used to see everything the same way but it's frustrating working with people who're still stuck in the old way. But you've kind of crossed the Rubicon and now you're stuck on the other side (laughs) ... kinda

lonely until you can convince some others to join you. The challenge was using the methodology to get them to see things differently too.

The tales of isolation and difficulty working with colleagues who don't 'get it' might make it seem that mindset change among leaders is going to be sporadic at best. However, the leader stories included a storytelling trope of attribution of responsibility and unity in which their persistence won the day and they won others over to the new mindset of organizing and leading. Interestingly, despite all the interviewed leaders telling of their own ah-ha! moments of insight, their descriptions of how other leaders made sense of the methodology did not contain the same sort of ah-ha! moments that they themselves had experienced:

DZ: ' - I may convince some, I may get some curious, but the only way of convincing them properly is for them to see themselves the effect that their current thinking, their current assumptions about design and management of work actually has on performance and on their people. That takes time'.

DJ, whose personal story included an ah-ha! moment within 45 minutes of hearing about the methodology, said:

> But I don't think it's ever going to be an instant road to Damascus experience for those that are participating, I think the best we can expect is to get people more curious ... personally I don't think you can learn (laughs) this method in three days and really understand the thinking behind the method, completely, within three days.

It's a One-Way Trip: You Can't Go from Knowledge Back to Ignorance

The leaders' stories about their change of thinking and how they championed this in their colleagues are described in a way that suggests some form of permanence or sustainability of their new mindset. Their story trope is of a one-way journey with no route back to the old way of thinking. This is a powerful story theme but my own experience working with leaders to coach them in the methodology was that some leaders who initially express an embracing of a new way of thinking following engagement with the methodology subsequently seem to revert to their previous modernist thinking about organization, change and leadership. So I wanted to explore with the group of leaders I was interviewing, who were all advocates of the methodology, how they sensemade the concept of this one-way journey that they were describing.

RW described it as like learning to walk – 'once you learn to walk you can't unlearn it. You can choose not to walk but you will always know that walking makes more sense so why wouldn't you?'. KB had a similar outlook – 'once you've got knowledge you can't go back to ignorance'. HR explained that as well as being a one-way journey, moving to a new mindset is not confined to organizational life – it affects your whole outlook:

> *HR:* I've also found that, and I mean this in the nicest possible way, that the transformation method I've found is a bit of a curse. There's no going back for me now, I can't go back to do the things that I used to do, and I certainly can't look at any customer experience that I have with any other company as a customer in the same way again'.

It seemed clear that the leaders sensemaking stories led to a sense of having crossed the Rubicon into a new mindset, a new perception of reality and that they felt that they could never go back to the frequently mentioned 'old world' or mindset.

Conclusions

The stories leaders recounted in their interviews produced four common themes and each of these are linked to concepts covered in my literature review and which I might expect to observe in my participant research as leaders sensemake their engagement with the postmodern methodology:

1. The importance of preunderstanding (Gummesson, 2000) in helping individuals contextualize and construct their sensemaking story of a journey from an old world to a new world (Balogun and Johnson, 2004, Gioia and Chittipeddi, 1991, Gioia and Thomas, 1996, Maitlis, 2005, Weick, 1988, 1993, 1995, 2005)
2. The drama of ah-ha! moments and cognitive dissonance (Beauvois and Joule, 1996, Festinger, 1957, 1964) when rationalizing is no longer an option and which leads to displaced concepts of leadership and organization (Schon, 1963, 1983) i.e. a new mindset
3. Heraclitan harmonizing of opposites (Chia, 1994, 1995, 1996, 1997, 1999, 2003, Graham, 2015) such as the description of rapid change in mindset which is described as both a long and slow process
4. Storytelling tropes (Gabriel, 2000) of attribution of responsibility and unity such as the leader as the hero fighting an ignorant collective opposition

The leaders' stories made sense to me and it seemed that my research should expect to find similar sensemaking happening with the leaders I work with. However, it is not quite that straightforward. My preunderstanding also told me that the stories I had been hearing were not universal. I have worked with leaders who engage with but then reject transformation methodologies and I have worked with leaders who initially tell similar enthusiastic stories but whose behaviors then seemed to more reflect their previous leadership style. As Argyris puts it, their espoused theories of action were incongruent with their theories-in-action (Argyris, 1976, 1980, 1990, 1993, 1994, 1995, 2004). I wanted to better understand this aspect of leader sensemaking in my research.

Something else struck me after I reflected on the stories leaders had told me. I realized that while they spent some time setting out their preunderstanding at the start of their stories, there was scant reference in their stories to some of the common change models or writers that practitioners tend to be familiar with (see my literature review in Chapter 1). There was no talk about Lewin's unfreezing and refreezing, nothing about Kotter's creating a sense of urgency or Kanter's guiding coalitions. Although I was not conscious of this during the interviews, it seemed surprising that such common models and recipes for change were not mentioned, even if just to discount them. However, this may have been a weakness of my interview structure in which I asked the leaders to focus on their making sense of the methodology and did not ask them to talk about existing change models with which they were familiar. Notwithstanding this, I was still a little surprised that in their fairly lengthy explanations of their preunderstanding none of the common business change models were mentioned.

Because the interviews were with leaders who had already made it clear they had 'got it' and were advocates of the methodology, they can only present a partial story of sensemaking and taken on their own could give a distorted view. The stories of enthusiastic advocates of the methodology and the new mindset it resulted in provided some pointers to look for in my participant observer research, but based on my previous experience of the more mixed reactions to the methodology, I set out to observe a fuller experience of leader sensemaking.

Note

1 SMART is a common organisational acronym usually meaning Specific, Measurable, Attainable, Reliable and Timed.

References

Argyris, C. 1976. Single-loop and double-loop models in research on decision making. *Administrative Science Quarterly*, Vol. 21, 363–375.

Argyris, C. 1980. Making the undiscussable and its undiscussability discussable. *Public Administration Review*, Vol. 40, 205–213.

Argyris, C. 1990. *Overcoming Organizational Defenses: Facilitating Organizational Learning*, MA, Allyn and Bacon.
Argyris, C. 1993. *Knowledge for Action: A Guide to Overcoming Barriers to Organizational Change*, San Fransisco, Jossey-Bass.
Argyris, C. 1994. Initiating change that perseveres. *Journal of Public Administration Research and Theory: J-PART*, Vol. 4, 343–355.
Argyris, C. 1995. Action science and organizational learning. *Journal of Managerial Psychology*, Vol. 10, 20–26.
Argyris, C. 2004. *Reasons and Rationalizations: The Limits to Organizational Knowledge*, Oxford, Oxford University Press.
Balogun, J. & Hope Hailey, V. 2004. *Exploring Strategic Change*, London, Prentice Hall.
Balogun, J. & Johnson, G. 2004. Organizational restructuring and middle manager sensemaking. *Academy of Management Journal*, Vol. 47, 523–549.
Beauvois, J.-L. & Joule, R.-V. 1996. *A Radical Dissonance Theory*, London, Taylor and Francis.
Blake, R. & Mouton, J. 1964. *The Managerial Grid: The Key to Leadership Excellence*, Houston, Gulf Publishing Co.
Chia, R. 1994. The Concept Of Decision: A Deconstructive Analysis. *Journal of Management Studies*, Vol. 31, 781–806.
Chia, R. 1995. From modern to postmodern organizational analysis. *Organization Studies*, Vol. 16, 579–604.
Chia, R. 1996. The problem of reflexivity in organizational research: Towards a postmodern science of organization. *Organization*, Vol. 3, 31–59.
Chia, R. 1997. Essai: Thirty years on: From organizational structures to the organization of thought. *Organization Studies*, Vol. 18, 685–707.
Chia, R. 1999. A 'rhizomic' model of organisational change and transformation: Perspective from a metaphsyics of change. *Annual British Academy of Management*, Vol. 10, 209–227.
Chia, R. 2003. Organization theory as a postmodern science. *In:* Tsoukas, H. & Knudsen, C. (eds.) *The Oxford Handbook of Organization Theory: Meta-Theoretical Perspectives*. Oxford: Oxford University Press.
Festinger, L. 1957. *A Theory of Cognitive Dissonance*, Stanford, Stanford University Press.
Festinger, L. 1964. Behavioral dupport for opinion change. *The Public Opinion Quarterly*, Vol. 28, 404–417.
Gabriel, Y. 2000. *Storytelling in Organizations: Facts, Fictions, and Fantasies*, Oxford, Oxford University Press.
Gioia, D. A. & Chittipeddi, K. 1991. Sensemaking and sensegiving in strategic change initiation. *Strategic Management Journal*, Vol. 12, 433–448.
Gioia, D. A. & Thomas, J. B. 1996. Identity, image, and issue interpretation: Sensemaking during strategic change in academia. *Administrative Science Quarterly*, Vol. 41, 370–403.
Graham, D. W. 2015. Heraclitus. *In:* Zalta, E. N. (ed.) *The Stanford Encyclopedia of Philosophy*. (Fall 2019 Edition). https://stanford.library.sydney.edu.au/archives/fall2019/
Gummesson, E. 2000. *Qualitative Methods in Management Research*, Thousand Oaks, Sage Publications.

Lewin, K. 1951. *Field Theory In Social Science*, New York, Harper & Brothers.
Maitlis, S. 2005. The social processes of organizational sensemaking. *Academy of Management Journal*, Vol. 48, 21–49.
Schon, D. A. 1963. *Displacement of Concepts*, London, Tavistock Publications.
Schon, D. A. 1983. *The Reflective Practitioner: How Professionals Think In Action*, London, Ashgate.
Siegal, W., Church, A. H., Javitch, M., Waclawski, J., Burd, S., Bazigos, M., Yang, T., Anderson-Rudolph, K. & Warner Burke, W. 1996. Understanding the management of change: An overview of managers' perspectives and assumptions in the 1990s. *Journal of Organizational Change Management*, Vol. 9, 54–80.
Weick, K. E. 1988. Enacted sensemaking In crisis situations. *Journal of Management Studies*, Vol. 25, 305–317.
Weick, K. E. 1993. The collapse of sensemaking in organizations: The Mann Gulch disaster. *Administrative Science Quarterly*, Vol. 38, 628–652.
Weick, K. E. 1995. *Sensemaking in Organizations*, London, Sage Publications.
Weick, K. E., Sutcliffe, K. M. & Obstfeld, D. 2005. Organizing and the process of sensemaking. *Organization Science*, Vol. 16, 409–421.

Part II

The Nine Elements of Leader Sensemaking

In the following chapters I explain each of the nine elements of leader sensemaking which I observed in my research. Before doing so I have some caveats to add.

Looking at each of the elements separately makes sense from the perspective of explaining each in detail, but it runs the risk of giving the impression that they operate independently when in fact they are closely inter-related. It also runs the risk that by presenting them in a sequence of chapters that the process of sensemaking itself is some sort of linear sequence of events. If only it were so simple. The reality is that any element can come into play at any time and in any order, and often in tandem with other elements at the same time. Notwithstanding the risks, I present to you the nine elements with the caveat that nothing should be read into the order in which I have chosen to present them to you.

I use many quotes from leaders I worked alongside. An ethics requirement of my research was that all leaders were promised that neither they or their organization would be identified and so names have been changed to protect anonymity. In my PhD Thesis I used exact verbatim quotes including discourse markers such as 'you know', pause fillers such as 'err' and 'um' and non-linguistic sounds that are familiar in conversations as 'coughs/laughs/sighed', and so forth. However, I have edited these out of the quotes in this book unless they seemed of significance in the verbal communication, for example where a pause, laugh or a repetition seemed to be being used for effect.

Before launching in to the nine elements of sensemaking I would like you to answer the following questions:

- Is the Earth round or flat?
- Does the sun revolve around the Earth or is it the Earth which revolves around the sun?

Actually you do not really need to think about the answers because by the time you finished reading each question had already answered it in your own mind by referencing your beliefs about such things. You cannot have helped but envisage a round or flat Earth, depending on which you believe to be true as you made sense of the question. I ask the questions because I will be using them in the following chapters and it will help you understand your own sensemaking process when you reflect back on the answers that popped into your head as you read them.

Finally, my research focuses on how leaders make sense of transformational change interventions. I was not trying to assess the success or failure of any particular change methodology or specific organizational intervention and so I simply refer to 'change methodology/ies' in the text. The sensemaking elements I have identified were common to all the leaders I worked with, whatever the particular change methodology being used.

With those caveats in mind I now describe the nine elements of leader sensemaking which I observed.

4 Ontology

Creating Realities

Ontology is not a word I heard any leader use in any of the research organizations, but it is a key aspect of leader sensemaking of change that I witnessed during my research. However, despite its key role I also learned that it is not necessarily the best place for a heretic to start when trying to influence the sensemaking of leaders engaging with a change methodology that challenges their existing paradigms. Notwithstanding what the leaders said about ah-ha! moments in Chapter 3, my research suggests that shifts in ontological perspectives follow on from, they don't drive, other sensemaking elements. It turns out that the other elements of sensemaking are better avenues to chip away at existing paradigms if you are to have any success at helping leaders adopt new ones.

I recently attended a meeting at which a leader gave a 20-minute talk about a proposed change initiative. He told his audience of fellow leaders that he would challenge and change what, during the presentation, he variously referred to as their paradigms, mindsets, mental models and thinking. In my experience it is not uncommon for leaders to treat these terms as some sort of shorthand for essentially the same thing, but the danger is that this then masks the scale of change in thinking that is being sought. Is a paradigm shift really the same as a change in mental models? To answer this we need to understand two key elements of leader sensemaking which involve branches of philosophy known as ontology and epistemology. Although there is some overlap between the two, at its simplest ontology can be thought of as our beliefs about what is true or real, whereas epistemology is concerned with our sources of knowledge that lead to and support our beliefs about reality. I will cover epistemology in a later chapter but for now will focus on ontology.

When I asked you if you believed the Earth to be round or flat the answer that popped into your head would tell me your ontological perspective – you are a round or flat Earther. You might have been thinking something along the lines of 'it's obvious – the Earth is (round or flat), in fact it's so obvious why would you even ask the question?'. Ontology raises basic questions about the nature of reality and the nature of the human being in the world. Burrell and Morgan (1979) argue that ontological assumptions relate to whether the phenomena under investigation exist independently of an individual or are the product of their consciousness; these assumptions query whether the:

> ... reality to be investigated is external to the individual – imposing itself on individual consciousness; whether "reality" is of an "objective" nature, or the product of individual consciousness; whether "reality" is a given "out there" in the world, or the product of one's mind.
>
> (Burrell and Morgan, 1979, p.1)

No matter whether you believe that the Earth is round or flat there is a good chance that you are what is termed a realist and share an objective perspective on reality along with other readers, i.e. the Earth, whatever shape you think it is, is a physical object independent of the person thinking about it. It exists, it is tangible, it is objective in nature.

But what about countries? They have borders, passports, economies, legal systems, citizens and other artefacts that prove their existence so you might believe countries to be tangible and objective in nature. However, if instead you hold a subjective perspective then you are a constructivist who does not believe that countries physically exist 'out there' but rather are a product of our own thinking. They are socially co-constructed entities that only exist as long as we continue to agree they do. History is a timeline of the coming together and disintegration of co-constructed realities that we call countries. The land and peoples and associated artefacts may be real but the constructs that we call countries are shifting sands over time.

So what about organizations – in what way do they exist? The answer again depends on your ontological perspective and either you will be a realist (they are tangible things) or constructivist (they are intangible co-created cognitive constructs that exist only as long as we will them to exist). I write this text in the midst of a global pandemic and deep recession. Organizations that 'existed' yesterday are gone today. All the tangible artefacts remain – the buildings, the equipment and resources, the staff, the stock, the customers. But the collective organizing activity that we called *the* organization has ceased. The organization that was socially co-created and imbued with physical artefacts has lost the collective will to continue organizing its existence and so now has become a memory.

Although organizations are social constructs that operate in an ever-changing environment, leaders also create some of the environment they must react to. As Weick (1995) puts it:

> ... there is *not* some kind of monolithic, singular, fixed environment that exists detached from and external to these people. Instead, in

> each case the people are very much a part of their own environments. They act, and in doing so create the materials that become the constraints and opportunities they face. There is not some impersonal 'they' who puts these environments in front of passive people. Instead, the 'they' is people who are more active. All too often people in organizations forget this. They fall victim to this blindspot because of an innocent sounding phrase, 'the environment'. The word *the* suggests something that is singular and fixed; the word *environment* suggests that this singular, fixed something is set apart from the individual. Both implications are nonsense.
>
> [Weick's italics] (p.31)

Constructivist reality is linked to the postmodern process ontology (Chia, 1994, 1995, 1996, 1997, 1999, 2003, Chia and Holt, 2006, MacLean et al., 2012) covered in Chapter 1. Weick argues that to be able to understand the social aspect of sensemaking we must be very careful about how we understand process. He quotes the work of Follett (1924, p.60) 'there is no result of process but only a moment in process'. In other words, discussion and interpretation of outcomes would more accurately be termed descriptions of moments in a process. Chia talks of organizations and leaders becoming, rather than being, which emphasizes these two things as verbs rather than nouns.

The sense leaders make of any change initiative is impacted by their ontological perspective and so the first step to engaging them is to try and understand their perspective and the level of challenge that any change you are proposing will present to them. Is the change at the level of their wider ontological perspective (the basic concepts and beliefs about the totality of reality), their current organizational or leadership paradigms (basic concepts and beliefs about a particular aspect of reality), specific and current mindsets (deeply held set of mental models), mental models (cognitive representations of specific aspects of the surrounding world, the relationships between its various parts and a person's intuitive perception about their own acts and their impacts) or day to day thinking (an ongoing aim-oriented flow of ideas and associations)? The transformational methodologies I was using in my research were most likely to impact leader paradigms and mindsets, but in so doing would have implications for their ontological perspectives.

The leaders I interviewed for Chapter 3 described their sensemaking as impacting their organizational and leadership paradigms. The frequent use of the language of old world, of crossing the Rubicon, and of a one-way journey from ignorance to knowledge imply a fundamental shift in thinking about organizational reality. Those leaders also talked about how their new organizational paradigm impacted their wider ontological perspective as they applied their new thinking to other aspects of their life.

The leaders I went on to work with during my research had previously engaged in a variety of change initiatives which focused on process and performance improvement – lean, business process re-engineering and six sigma. These are all examples of approaches in which the main input is detailed process redesign and which involve some changes in mental models but can leave current leader paradigms intact with the inevitable reimposition of the thinking that drove the desire for change in the first place. Seddon describes such lean methods as a 'wicked disease' (Seddon, 2010) because they are adopted by leaders without the necessary understanding of the thinking behind them. A criticism often leveled at lean methodologies is that western leaders traveled to Japan in the 1970s to learn what they were doing that had transformed their industries from a byword for poor quality into producing world beating quality products that were decimating western industries. Those leaders came back with a series of lean 'tools' that they had seen in operation and went about applying them in their own businesses. But the leaders had failed to learn the most important thing about lean – the thinking behind the ways of organizing and leading that resulted in the tools they were frequently unsuccessfully trying to apply in their own organizations. Many of the leaders I worked with during my research had experienced the wicked disease and, because they had not delivered their planned outcomes, were now seeking to explore if they should engage with more radical transformation methodologies. But of course they started this exploration from within their existing ontological perspective and associated leadership paradigms. I assumed that all the leaders would be firm realists in their thinking about change, organizations and leadership as objective things and indeed this seemed to be the case. At one point I tried to challenge the concept of organization as a noun with a group of leaders and the director of the legal department politely pointed out to me that *'whilst that's an interesting philosophical perspective it's somewhat out of touch with reality since UK companies ... actually in all the countries we operate in ... have a legal status of independent.. albeit it non-human ... person with rights, duties and obligations'*. Her reality was rooted in her understanding of the legal status of *the* organization and she sensed any challenge to that as unrealistic.

Most leaders talked about *the* organization as if it was some sort of independent actor. Those same leaders whose collective decisions determined the decisions and activities of the company nevertheless talked about *the* company/organization as if it made decisions independently of them. In one organization I was introducing leaders to the Beyond Budgeting concept which encourages organizations to abandon traditional budgeting and focus on adaptive leading and organizing processes. The response was almost unanimous scorn, but this was presented in the form of '**the** business would never wear it even if it was something that was remotely possible' and '**it's** [the business] been using the same financial model for 300 years and **it's** not going to commit suicide for the sake of some trendy fad' (my emphasis).

Why this talk of a concrete 'the'? My first interpretation was that this was a case of leaders consciously avoiding expressing opposition to a concept by projecting that opposition onto an objectified organization (by objectified I mean a social construct expressed in a concrete form). During 10 years of research in various organizations I frequently and consistently came across similar examples even when there was no major issue of contention and which suggest that perhaps it was not a conscious act but rather a subconscious perception of reality. As a practitioner and researcher I see here the Parmenidean mindset reflected in what I would interpret as the development of Scientific Management and modernist thinking of organizations as stable entities. Chia argues that in the neo-Parmenidean world-view '... an organization is deemed to exist relatively independently of the individual actors associated with it and therefore form an appropriate theoretical object of analysis' (Chia, 2003, p.119).

Wood argues that leadership similarly suffers from the view of leaders as objects of analysis and argues for Chia's becoming rather than being, postmodern perspective:

> ... process studies seek to elucidate the ongoing nature of reality. They give primacy to inter-relatedness and flux, ahead of the materialistic belief in the nature of things. Looked at this way, leadership is better seen as a system of mutual dependence, rather than a self-evident entity ... [and] process studies place emphasis on understanding how leadership comes to be rather than what it is.
>
> (Wood, 2005, p.24)

This view of the ongoing nature of reality moves research away from organization as the object of study and the leader as the change agent to an understanding of the interdependence of leadership and organizing activity in an environment of never ceasing turbulence:

> What this means is that 'organizational change' is not something that needs deliberate intervention or orchestration. Instead, merely *relaxing* the deeply entrenched organizational and institutionalized habits, which keep 'organizations' together and which enable them to be thought of as 'thing-like', is itself sufficient to allow change to occur of its own volition.
>
> (Chia, 1999, p.225)

The idea that change does not need to be 'led' is likely to present a considerable challenge to leaders used to enacting planned or emergent change models, but it is not a new idea. The Organizational Development movement which developed from the 1980s onwards includes a stream that seeks to change mindsets and consciousness as the principle method to address change dynamics and that transformation requires a change in consciousness, often starting with the leadership (Marshak and Grant, 2008). Clegg and Walsh (2004) argue that the management of change is characterized as attempting to replace a dominant paradigm/mindset with a new one. The leaders in the research organizations were exploring the option of engaging in just such paradigm/mindset replacement with a variety of postmodern influenced transformation methodologies including systems thinking, agile and beyond budgeting. I say influenced because although none of these methodologies were explicitly postmodern their underlying principles reflected essential elements of postmodern organizational theory:

1. Change is seen as the norm, not an epiphenomenon. This aspect aligns with Heraclitan flux or the constant stream of experience in sensemaking.
2. Leaders cannot manage change – rather they need to recognize the inevitability and unpredictability of it and be agile enough to react and adapt to it. However, the act of reacting influences and creates new problems (environment) which they must in turn react and adapt to. This cycle never ceases.
3. Leadership is not a thing, it is a result of complex relationships and leaders must give up their current paradigms and mindsets about leadership in organizations. The business methodologies were aligned with Burns' (1978) concept of transforming leadership rather than the subsequently developed concept of *the* transformational leader.
4. Organizations are not things, they are methods of coping with complexity and chaos and seeing them as such allows us to move to more agile and adaptable organizational designs and structures.

It might seem that if leaders had decided to explore the possibilities of these transformation methodologies then their sensemaking must have already resulted in them feeling that their current paradigms or mindsets were flawed. However, such an assumption would be wrong as it is based on the premise that the leaders understood that the methodologies would challenge their current paradigms. They did not. I was faced with one of two situations when first engaging with leaders during my research, the first was that they had heard something about the transformation methodologies being applied in other organizations and what appealed to them was the results that those organizations had achieved. They were curious, but they showed little understanding about the principles behind the transformation methodologies. The second situation was that leaders had been instructed to engage with the transformation methodology by leaders above them in the hierarchy, although this was frequently talked about as 'the' organization having decided that leaders would engage with the methodology whether they wished to or not.

In both cases my active participant role was to help leaders make sense of the transformation methodology and to help them get to a point where they agreed to engage with the methodology, with the ultimate goal that they would embrace a new paradigm of organizing and leading. This left the question of by what method leaders can be moved from old to new paradigm? Early in my research I assumed that the best place to start was to address the ontological issues at the outset. After all, the leaders interviewed in Chapter 3 all had their ah-ha! moments in an initial presentation about the new methodology so what better place to start? The problem is that this assumes that sensemaking is a rational and logical process which can be done in a meeting or training room through the presentation of data and logical argument. Despite the stories of the leaders in Chapter 3 this is not the case. The reason why will become clearer in subsequent chapters.

Not only did my attempts at engaging leaders in discussion and reflection on the ontological perspectives of the transformation methodologies not result in any obvious ah-ha! moments, it actually seemed to generate skepticism or antagonism. In my own retrospective sensemaking it seems somewhat naïve to think that I could convince leaders in a short presentation that their fundamental beliefs about organizational reality are flawed. What sense would you make of me giving you a one-hour presentation that your thinking about Earth being round/flat is wrong and that the opposite is true? I think it unlikely that your response would be 'oh ok, clearly I've been wrong all along' and the leaders were no different. Typical reactions included:

> *you're hardly in the door but it's like you're telling us that we don't know how to run the business*

> *we've been very successful for many years but you want me to believe we've been doing it wrong all this time*

> *What planet are these people* [designers of the methodology] *from? … I mean really, this stuff is all a bit mumbo jumbo … it's out of touch with reality*

> *You people are a cult and it's like you're trying to convert us to a new religion*

It became clear that that leaders are best helped to make sense of new paradigms or mindsets not by confronting them with the enormity of the change in thinking required but instead by chipping away at their current thinking by first arousing their curiosity and then gaining their agreement to engage in activities that allow them to challenge their current thinking – what Beauvois and Joule (1996) call induced compliance in counter-attitudinal behaviors, supplemented by guided reflexive practice that gives leaders an opportunity to challenge their current thinking, identify alternatives and experiment with applying their new thinking. My new sense was that trying to get leaders to sense that the methodology was about mindset change not process improvement when they had not yet engaged, or even committed to engage, with the methodology would create confusion. However, I also felt that focusing on practical application of the methodology was exactly the reason that leaders sensemaking of it was of process improvement. It seemed to me that compresence of opposites (this element is covered in Chapter 11) was needed if the leaders were to understand what they were being asked to commit to. So I first sought to give them preunderstanding (this element is covered in Chapter 7) of application of the methodology in diverse types of business areas using my own experience and which I thought would enhance my credibility as an expert with whom they could commit to work. Secondly, after establishing the methodology had practical application in any business area, I then sought to give leaders a sense of the importance of their own thinking and mindset in determining the outcomes of engaging with the methodology.

There is no magic recipe for achieving the correct balance of pragmatism and discussion of ontology and I learned the importance of listening for cues from leader language. Leaders with a modernist ontology of change as an epi-phenomenon often find the outcomes that the methodology has delivered in other organizations that they have heard about appealing but think of it as a change project that can be delegated to a project manager to implement. A common example of this was the two most frequently asked questions by leaders thinking of engaging with the methodology. These were what organizational benefits will it deliver (payoff)? and how long will it take (timescale)?

From within their existing perspective these were not unreasonable questions but a fully transparent answer from within the perspective of the methodologies is 'no one can tell'. My experience was that this sort of answer did not facilitate initial engagement of leaders as typified in the response from RU, a director, *you can't seriously expect me to sign a blank cheque? You know how this organization works and I have to have a business case with a tight cost/benefit analysis ... so there's no way I can sign up to something that has no timescale and no figures on the payoff.* In another organization I was approached by a senior leader who was pulling together a report for the board on the transformation intervention which was being proposed. He asked me for figures on how long the intervention would take and what savings it would deliver. When I explained that while from experience I could give examples of how long similar exercises had taken in other organizations and the results that they had achieved we would have to add a caveat that we could not safely predict that these would apply in this case. His response was *no, no, that's not going to stand up. They expect hard figures and they have to show the savings are significantly greater than the costs. Just give me some figures that you think sound realistic and I'll use them in the report.* I was taken aback and said surely he didn't want to go to the board with spurious figures but he said *no one will check if they were met anyway, and if they did it would be no different from most other projects – virtually none are ever delivered on time or in budget.* I refused so the Director made up his own figures for the report. When I discussed what had happened with another senior leader who was involved in deciding whether to proceed with the intervention he responded in conspiratorial tones that seemed to demonstrate defensive reasoning in his sensemaking (covered in Chapter 10) *you seem surprised but it's quite common ... everyone knows that most reports have made up figures to back up their recommendations ... coz he's right ... getting anything done takes so [expletive] long that even if anyone did look back at the original figures all the people involved will probably have moved on or will have their backs well covered about why they didn't work out.* So, I asked, is the de facto policy here essentially just make up figures? and was told *pretty much but you do have to have to make it look credible. Don't expect anyone to admit to doing it though ...* (tapped side of his nose with index finger) *you ain't seen me, right?(laughs)* [this was the catchphrase of a popular but dubious sketch show character at the time].

The predictable questions and the behaviors of the leaders reveal a Parmenidean, modernist, project management mindset about change. In this mindset, change is seen as an epiphenomenon for which you can identify specific outcomes in advance and which can be carefully managed using key dates, milestones, costs and deadlines, and so forth. From a more processual perspective, this modernist thinking contributes to, and explains, research findings (Balogun and Hope Hailey, 2004, Siegal et al., 1996) that between 70% and 90% of change 'programs' fail to deliver the planned outcomes. A postmodern ontology recognizes that continuous flux is reality and any outcome set in advance will be obsolete almost as soon as it has been set. There was an unspoken sense of the futility in specifying outcomes in the request of the leader who asked me to make up some figures for his report and his comment that projects never met budget or timescale targets. However, rather than questioning the setting of planned outcomes, leaders engaged in single loop learning solutions that involved playing the system and making up figures that 'worked'.

After my lack of success trying to get leaders to challenge ontological perspective at initial engagement I tried a more pragmatic approach using some of the other elements of sensemaking – involving identifying and creating leader preunderstanding of the methodology (covered in Chapter 7) and encouraging commitment compliance (covered in Chapter 9). This approach created curiosity and proved more successful in helping leaders make initial sense of engaging with transformation. However, I did not want them making sense of it as a change project so I touched on the ontological implications by using an introductory statement along the lines of:

> We are where we are. Everything about the way we organize is done for a good reason and we are not going to waste time using hindsight to try and blame anyone for the fact that the environment has changed. We will be using a new lens to understand the thinking that led to where we are and question whether it is still appropriate. The methodology is based on the premise that 'stuff happens and it happens all the time'. Thinking that was appropriate several years ago, or one year ago, or even yesterday, may not be the right thinking today. So our focus is to look forward and constantly monitor that our thinking and way we organize are right for the environment we are in today, then tomorrow and every day moving forward.

It is also worth noting that while the strength of leader modernist ontology was evident, there were nevertheless indications that elements of postmodern ontology did exist and which offered hope that all was not lost. When working for a Canadian organization I was traveling on the Metro in Toronto and saw an advert by Advertising Standards Canada which read *Advertising is subjective. The truth isn't. Truth in advertising matters*. The creator of the advertisement would appear to be an objectivist. This view of *the* truth as being objective in nature mirrors what I experienced in the research organizations. A common objective of leaders was establishing the **one** source of truth in the form of a single and universal source of data. It reflects the view that management information and data might be subjectively interpreted but that nevertheless a single source of true data exists.

However, when I was discussing my research with GP, a leader in one of the insurance companies I worked in, I told him about the advert I'd seen in Canada and explained how I thought this could be a metaphor for the 'one source of truth' belief in organizations and his response was interesting:

GP: ... that one source of truth stuff is bullshit.. the thing is ... well it's more like sort of .... mmm, ok Ron, we talk about the one truth kinda thing but there isn't one. Like, hmm, we've got a customer who has a basket of polices with us and so we give him a discount

[on] each one.. you know, coz he's given us the lot. But then at renewal someone gives him a cheaper quote and so he takes a couple of them off to [competitor]. Naturally we say ok buddy you're not giving us all your business now so you're not getting your discount anymore coz you don't qualify. Perfectly fair and reasonable yeah? But the customer runs [to] the regulator and says they're punishing me for shopping around and bullying me and so they're being anti-competitive.. sort of crap coz he's pissed he's lost his discount. He says he hasn't made any claims and his risk hasn't increased but we're increasing the price we were happy to take before. So we tell the regulator of course we're not punishing him, the discount was a reward for giving us all his business and we're just reflecting the correct competitive price now that he doesn't qualify for the reward. The regulator's job is to decide the truth. Trouble is we both think we're telling it as it is. The regulator isn't finding the truth… he's just deciding which one he prefers! …. Sometimes we're lucky it's ours … yeah? … but sometimes he sides with the politicians or whoever is putting the pressure on him and decides it's theirs.

GP is suggesting there is no objective truth, indeed there can be two opposing truths at the same time – the reasonable insurer who is removing a discount because of the customer has broken the terms and the bullying and anti-competitive insurer who is punishing the customer for shopping around. Like Schrodinger's cat which can be considered both dead and alive until the box is opened and we find out which it is, both the customer's and the organization's versions of what is going on are true until the regulator chooses which it is to be. GP was not the only leader who sensed truth as subjective.

When I was working with the senior actuaries in a large financial services organization which was making much of its 'one source of truth' policy and practices it struck me as odd that the organization was presenting different performance figures to different groups of stakeholders. My assumption was that the explanation must be that the data were being interpreted differently by different people as they presented it to various stakeholders. I discussed this with SM the Director, himself an actuary, and he surprised me with a somewhat subjectivist perspective:

SM: No I don't think it's an issue of interpretation of the data at all. If it was then there'd be an issue of accuracy. No, the fact is that the regulator and the markets and internal leaders all have different views of the world and so necessarily the data they want and get is different too. They're all looking at the same thing but there's [sic] multiple realities because essentially there's three different organizations – a sort of internal one that leaders are here to

> run, the external one that customers and shareholders care about and the legal/regulatory one that the regulator cares about, and that's ok. Each one's different but it's still true.

These examples of multiple truths and realities suggest sensemaking is more nuanced than compartmentalizing leaders as having either a modernist or a postmodernist perspective. Leader sensemaking is complex and the other eight elements all strengthen and weaken commitment to existing paradigms and mindsets. In the following chapters I explain the paradox of how sensemaking elements can both reinforce and undermine ontological perspectives – often both at the same time.

Given the all-encompassing nature of ontological perspective it is unlikely that an interventionist directly challenging a leader's ontological perspective will prove a successful strategy. I said that there is no sequence of sensemaking, but there is an element of ontological perspective changes emerging from an interventionist influencing the eight sensemaking elements in the following chapters in order to introduce and then build on elements of doubt.

References

Balogun, J. & Hope Hailey, V. 2004. *Exploring Strategic Change*, London, Prentice Hall.

Beauvois, J.-L. & Joule, R.-V. 1996. *A Radical Dissonance Theory*, London, Taylor and Francis.

Burns, J. M. 1978. *Leadership*, New York, Harper and Row.

Burrell, G. & Morgan, G. 1979. *Sociological Paradigms and Organizational Analysis*, Oxford, Heinemann.

Chia, R. 1994. The concept of decision: A deconstructive analysis. *Journal of Management Studies*, Vol. 31, 781–806.

Chia, R. 1995. From modern to postmodern organizational analysis. *Organization Studies*, Vol. 16, 579–604.

Chia, R. 1996. The problem of reflexivity in organizational research: Towards a postmodern science of organization. *Organization*, Vol. 3, 31–59.

Chia, R. 1997. Essai: Thirty years on: From organizational structures to the organization of thought. *Organization Studies*, Vol. 18, 685–707.

Chia, R. 1999. A 'rhizomic' model of organisational change and transformation: Perspective from a metaphsyics of change. *British Journal of Management*, Vol. 10, 209–227.

Chia, R. 2003. Organization theory as a postmodern science. *In:* Tsoukas, H. & Knudsen, C. (eds.) *The Oxford Handbook of Organization Theory: Meta-Theoretical Perspectives*. (pp. 113–142). Oxford: Oxford University Press.

Chia, R. & Holt, R. 2006. Strategy as practical coping: A Heideggarian perspective. *Organization Studies*, Vol. 27, 635–655.

Clegg, C. & Walsh, S. 2004. Change management: Time for change! *European Journal of Work and Organizational Psychology*, Vol. 13, 217–239.

Follett, M. P. 1924. *Creative Experience*, New York, Longmans, Green.

Maclean, M., Harvey, C. & Chia, R. 2012. Sensemaking, storytelling and the legitimization of elite business careers. *Human Relations*, Vol. 65, 17–40.

Marshak, R. J. & Grant, D. 2008. Organizational discourse and new organization development practices. *British Journal of Management*, Vol. 19, S7–S19.

Seddon, J. 2010. Lean is a wicked disease: How service organisations are waking up to the problem. *Vanguard-method Newsletter* [Online]. Available from: www.vanguard-method.net [Accessed 30th June 2012].

Siegal, W., Church, A. H., Javitch, M., Waclawski, J., Burd, S., Bazigos, M., Yang, T., Anderson-Rudolph, K. & Warner Burke, W. 1996. Understanding the management of change: An overview of managers' perspectives and assumptions in the 1990s. *Journal of Organizational Change Management*, Vol. 9, 54–80.

Weick, K. E. 1995. *Sensemaking in Organizations*, London, Sage Publications.

Wood, M. 2005. *The Fallacy of Misplaced Leadership. Centre for Leadership Studies*, Exeter, University of Exeter.

5 Storytelling

If You're Going to Tell a Story, Make It a Good One

Stories and fables have long been used as a vehicle for communication in many popular business publications aimed at managers and leaders. Business parables and fables such as Who Moved My Cheese? (Johnson, 1998), The Goal (Goldratt and Cox, 1984) and Fish! (Lundin et al., 2000) have sold millions of copies and have remained in the business book bestseller lists since being published. Academic writers also find storytelling to be a relevant organizational research technique as exemplified by 'Telling Fairy Tales in the Boardroom' (Kets De Vries, 2015).

The OED (2015) defines a story as

> A narrative, true *or presumed to be true*, relating to important events and celebrated persons of a more or less remote past; a historical relation or anecdote. (my italics)

Gabriel (2000) argues that:

> It is now widely agreed that stories are part of a sensemaking process that can be researched *in situ*, without that burdensome requirement of social science research – the need to establish the validity of claims, the facts behind allegations, the truth behind the tales. For, as it has been widely argued, the truth of a story lies not in *the facts*, but in *the meaning*. (author's italics)
>
> (Gabriel, 2000, p.4)

However, notwithstanding that in stories truth may lie in meaning rather than facts, as a researcher I have striven in my own sensemaking to balance an understanding of the facts as they seem and the meaning with which they are imbued. My ethnographic research study was itself a story of what was observed and the meaning with which I have imbued it. As Gabriel points out, formal reports and research documents 'do not merely furnish the material for stories, but, in as much as they make sense, *are* stories' (Gabriel, 2000, p.17).

Boje emphasizes the importance of organizational storytelling:

> In organisations, storytelling is the preferred sensemaking currency of human relationships among internal and external stakeholders … it is the institutional memory system of the organisation.
>
> (Boje, 1991, p.106)

Gabriel recognizes these links between storytelling and interpretation, and therefore of sensemaking, when arguing that it is reflexive interpretation:

> It is reflexive, in the sense of continuously recreating the past according to the present, interpretations becoming stories in their own right. It is interactive in the sense that most stories are multi-authored, with organizational members alternating in the roles of teller and listener, adding 'factual' cues or interpretive twists as a story unravels. It is dialogical, in that the truth of the story lies not in any one variant as in the process through which the text emerges.
>
> (Gabriel, 2000, p.18)

Gabriel (2000, p.36) identifies eight poetic tropes which he argues are 'the storyteller's central interpretive devices':

- Attribution of motive (to a seemingly motiveless event)
- Attribution of causal connections (linking coincidental events as causal or related)
- Attribution of responsibility, namely, blame and credit (casting others as heroes or villains)
- Attribution of unity (stereotyping classes of people as an undifferentiated entity of others e.g. 'them' or 'they')
- Attribution of fixed qualities, especially in opposition (often linked to 'they' or 'them' e.g. they lied once so they always lie)
- Attribution of emotion (presenting people as extremes in order to bring into relief the behavior of others e.g. the panicking of others versus the calm hero)
- Attribution of agency (turning something passive or inanimate into something active e.g. 'the organization' becomes an active (usually negative) actor in many stories)
- Attribution of providential significance (imbuing random events with fateful significance or divine providence)

Each one of these tropes serves two possible purposes – as a way of making sense of specific parts of a narrative or for making connections between different parts of the narrative. The tropes are used to support particular interpretations and thus are an important element of retrospective sensemaking in which, like Garfinkel's juror's (1967, p.114) who decided guilt or innocence first and then spent their deliberations trying to justify their decision, the outcome comes before the decision. In storytelling, the tropes are used to support and justify an interpretation already made of events (I discuss interpretation in Chapter 13). However, they are used selectively and are seldom stated explicitly. One has to listen carefully to understand how the story you are being told has been, or is being, crafted.

But there is another element to leader sensemaking stories – no one likes a boring story. Which is why leaders exciting stories can sometimes seem at odds with my observations of how they made sense of what was happening. Weick (1995), one of the key writers on sensemaking, argues that it is essentially about story construction. Sensemaking is something that:

> ... preserves plausibility and coherence, something that is reasonable and memorable, something that embodies past experience and expectations, something that resonates with other people, something that can be constructed retrospectively but also can be used prospectively, something that captures both feeling and thought, something that allows for embellishment to fit current oddities, something that is fun to construct. In short, what is necessary in sensemaking is a good story.
>
> (p.60)

Attributions of Significance and ah-ha! Moments

All the leaders interviewed in Chapter 3 talked about ah-ha! moments from attending presentations or workshops but in all my work with leaders I seldom observed behaviors or communication that suggested any sort of ah-ha! moment during introductory presentations. However, they did surface in the sensemaking stories of leaders *after* they had engaged with the methodology and *after* the leaders had completed the action learning and critical reflexivity phase and moved into experimenting with new ways of thinking and leading. What is curious is that frequently when leaders start talking about their ah-ha! moments they place them much earlier in time in their stories than when they first start talking about them.

In one organization I attended a meeting of senior leaders at which one, SW, was describing his experience of engaging with the business change methodology. He made several references during the meeting to his 'epiphany' when he suddenly realized that his current thinking about how to be a leader was 'all wrong'. I had been working with SW for four months and while I felt his mindset had changed over that period, I couldn't recall any particular moment when he expressed a sudden insight such as he was describing in the meeting. So I wanted to ask him about his epiphany, which he was clearly using in the sense of 'an illuminating discovery, realization, or disclosure' (Merriam-Webster, 2017).

After the meeting finished I spoke to SW and said I wanted to better understand the moments of insight that leaders talked about and asked if I could discuss the epiphany moment he had talked about in the meeting:

Me: you said you had your epiphany during the data gathering exercise when you were mapping the flows and were shocked to discover the waste and duplication going on?

SW: yeah it was mind-blowing and a complete shock to me. You think you know as a leader how things work but when you're confronted with proof that you don't it shakes you to the core. That was the point when I realized that my thinking was way out of line with reality.

Me: was this at the end once the mapping was complete or during the process?

SW: hmm good question. I think it really hit me about half way through when we did the complex quote process. I'd seen some of the waste in the other processes but I assumed that the complex one was more slick. But when we lifted that rock and had a look underneath and it became obvious it was just as bad, if not worse, than the others that's when it hit me.

Me: you say it hit you but I'm trying to understand what that actually means. This morning you told the others it was an epiphany which makes it seem like quite a dramatic moment?

SW: well it was dramatic for me because I suddenly realized my thinking was wrong and what I thought I knew I didn't at all. I remember when you were first telling me about your PhD and you talked about reality and how [the methodology] gives us a sort of different lens way to view reality. Well this [his epiphany moment] is when I got what you meant by that. I saw so clearly that what I thought was the reality of the [name of business unit] business was an illusion and the real reality was quite shocking really. Obviously the old system seems pretty lunatic now, but we'd never seen it up to then. So I think yeah that was the moment when I was thinking 'wow – how wrong was I?'

Me: that's interesting and very similar to what other leaders have described to me. But what's interesting is that it's very hard to see these important moments in action. We've been working together on this intervention and of course we were working together on the mapping but I can't recall hearing you cry out Eureka! (laughs). So you kept your epiphany to yourself (laughs). Did you talk about it at the time to anyone else or do you think it's an internal thing?

SW: hmm I'm not sure ...(thinking)... I remember being very shocked and I thought I was quite vocal about that (laughs). Wasn't I?

Me: oh we both talked about how bad the data was but I just mean I don't remember you saying that it was such a shock to you or you using the term epiphany at that time and I'm wondering if you realized at that time just how important a moment it was or if it was only afterwards that it dawned on you?

SW: oh right. I maybe didn't say much at the time because I was still kind of coming to terms with it. And actually there's something in what you say ... although I still think that was the time I saw things differently. But maybe I didn't talk about it until I'd thought about it a bit more. Certainly it became sort of more crystallized nearer the end of the intervention as we thought through what we'd found. But that mapping was the point where I 'got it' for sure.

On one hand SW was quite clear about a specific moment when he had his epiphany but on the other, when questioned to think about it becomes a bit less definite and senses that there was a process of reflection which led him to realize this was the epiphany. SW seemed to be sensemaking that he had had an epiphany but didn't know it at the time and he only realized it was an epiphany later after he decided it had happened. Despite his firm belief that the mapping of one particular flow was when he 'got it' and had his ah-ha! moment, upon reflection he also thinks he was still coming to terms with what he'd found at that time and it was only retrospectively that he could be sure that was it. This is in line with sensemaking theory which stresses its retrospective nature and the concept that interpretation involves the creation of that which we then interpret. I reflected on what SW told me and my own sensemaking was that perhaps SW's reality creation followed a sequence of interpreting his shock at what he was finding as something significant and then subsequently interpreting this significance as an ah-ha! moment. He then wove this interpreted ah-ha! moment into his sensemaking story that he shared with others and in the story the ah-ha! moment now came to happen and be recognized as such at the same moment in time.

Tipping Points

In another intervention, SH frequently mentioned at meetings that he had reached a 'tipping point' which happened early on in the intervention and as he saw some of the financial data that they were gathering. Tipping Point is a bestselling book by Gladwell (2000) and I have heard other leaders use the phrase in the same context as SH, i.e. a specific point and insight that leads them to change their thinking. It seems to me that SH and the others were using the phrase tipping point in the sense of an individual ah-ha! moment rather than Gladwell's concept of a collective tipping point in society. As with SW's sensemaking story, SH's tipping point was quite specific and, perhaps not surprisingly given his role, was when he saw financial data. I asked him about what it was that caused it.

Me: I'm very interested in the tipping point that you've talked about. Can I ask you how it happened?

SH: I think I've said before that it was the data that did it for me. I'm a naturally conservative person and I didn't buy into [the methodology] at the outset. I understood what it was trying to achieve but I would say my position was that I was in the shop but not ready to buy. Then we started to gather the financial data and at first I thought it was not so surprising really. I knew there would be some problems and I didn't expect everything to be exactly as I'd expected. But as more and more of our findings kind of contradicted what I was expecting I began to get quite concerned. At first I thought maybe we were doing something wrong. You know Ron that I'm very much a detail person and so I spent a long time going over the detail to see what we were doing wrong. Of course I couldn't find anything wrong and so that for me was the tipping point. Once I had the detail and the data to back it up, I knew that we were in a very different situation than I'd imagined up to that point. I guess the shop till was ringing as I bought the goods (laughs).

Me: Yeah that makes sense. As you say, you're a very detail person so I wondered when you talked about tipping points what stage the detail tipped you over?

SH: Well ..... I'm not sure that it was one spreadsheet that did it. I'd been getting more and more frustrated with the games that [names of two other senior leaders] were playing and I knew their figures were fanciful but it was when we gathered our data and I'd checked it to be absolutely sure that I knew we were in a whole new ball game. That was the tipping point because now I knew we were in a position to really challenge the way we are approaching transformation and that kills our current mentality about how we organize this place.

Me: But I've only heard you talking about it being the tipping point in the last couple of weeks so did it take a little while for you to realize the significance of the data?

SH: Well it's my cautious nature and I wanted to check it myself first so I did that and only then did I believe it. But I'm a cautious person, I think I just said that didn't I? (laughs) ... so it took me a little while to say it was definitely my tipping point.

SH's description of his tipping point is similar to SW's. When he was telling others about it he was clear that it was a single moment in time but when I asked him to think carefully about when it happened and when he realized it had happened, he identified a gap because he had taken time to reflect on what he thought he was seeing and wanted to be absolutely sure. It was only later once he had convinced himself that he had seen what he thought he had seen that he reached his tipping point, but his sensemaking story moved the tipping point back to his seeing of the original data, not after his careful scrutiny of it.

BE, the CEO in another of the research organizations claimed that he had witnessed a collective ah-ha! He said that he felt there had been a moment of insight for many leaders at a two-day event for senior leaders held two weeks previously when he had used a messy slide showing all the connections between different departments of the organization and the number of different people/units a customer had to deal with. I had called it the spaghetti slide because it looked like a plate of spaghetti to me but BE said 'we had a real insight moment on the second day and it was the Bolognese slide that did it'. He was saying that this slide was some form of ah-ha! moment in a collective sensemaking setting. But what intrigued me was that this was not a new slide. It had been used and presented to the same group of people three months previously and went completely unremarked or commented on. Now it was being retrospectively extracted from the event two weeks earlier and called out as a collective ah-ha! moment. The first thing that made me curious was how such an apparently significant slide went virtually unnoticed three months earlier. However, even if it had been 'missed' in some way I was also curious that BE felt that the second sighting of the slide had triggered a collective ah-ha! moment that led to a questioning of mindsets when this was the first mention of the slide that I had heard from any of the participants at either of the events at which it had been used. I raised it in the discussion:

Me: I'm glad the Bolognese slide had such an impact but to be honest it's not the one that I would have thought would be most remembered. But one thing I've learned in my research is that the most important moments for leaders can't be predicted and are often the most surprising. The thing is, I didn't see that it had any significance for those in the room a fortnight ago. Why do you think it was so significant?

BE: Oh it was significant alright. I could see people squirming in their seats when they saw the mess we've created and that most of them are trying their damndest to protect. I think they could see that this was going to be untenable moving forward because nobody in their right mind can say that that mess is justifiable. You could cut the tension in the room with a knife (laughs).

Me: Interesting! None of them has said anything to me, has anyone talked about it to you?

BE: I've spoken to [names a few of the participants] and they have talked about the overall presentation and how powerful it was.

Me: What's really interesting is that the slide isn't new. It was presented three months ago and didn't raise an eyebrow (laughs). It was in the Mgt Team event just after you started.

BE: Really? Well I guess minds weren't as focused on how real and dramatic the changes were going to be then. I'm surprised I didn't pick up on it but maybe I was just storing it for future use when the time was right and it [meeting two weeks ago] was right and it certainly made an impact this time.

After the meeting I discussed this with another leader and I said I didn't recall any particular reaction to the slide at either meeting and his response was:

LY: I think BE already knew about the 'spaghetti' so it's hard to believe that it came as a bolt out of the blue to him and I think it's more that he realized it's a really useful slide to summarize the mess our current thinking is causing and a handy stick to beat those who aren't getting it. I'm not so sure anyone else got the significance of it – until BE started talking about it and making it significant. Still ... makes a good story!

I asked him if he meant that there was no ah-ha! moment for BE and the other leaders and he said his sense was that BE really believes it was an insight moment for him but actually BE had only come to that conclusion after two weeks of trying to rationalize what he had heard. So the collective ah-ha! moment seems more like an example of BE retrospectively creating significance for something he had seen and heard at least twice in a period of three months. His sensemaking included a clear view that others shared his ah-ha! moment, but no one else had observed this. LY's comment that 'still ... makes a good story' seems to me to capture the essence of the reason for the appearance of ah-ha! moments at the time they appear. The retrospective interpretation and subsequent sensemaking is a response to, and a solution for, the cognitive dissonance they are experiencing *after* engaging with the methodology. It 'explains' to the leader why they have committed to new ways of thinking and new behaviors that they are engaging in. A sensemaking story with the drama of ah-ha! moments makes sense to leaders trying to understand the challenges to their current thinking. As I reflected on this, I came across a networking colleague who was also reflecting on similar observations and who summed it up well:

> There seem to be times when a number of things come together unexpectedly and without even realizing you've been pondering them and all of a sudden you get a sense of connection for which the only meaningful response seems to be Whoa!
>
> (Bellinger, 2017)

In conclusion, storytelling is an integral aspect of sensemaking but is only one element of it and does not have to be empirically accurate for it to be real for leaders. In Chapter 13 I will explore post-engagement sensemaking stories of leaders in which all the elements are pulled together to create plausible 'good' sensemaking stories and which can provide simultaneously helpful and unhelpful preunderstanding for those thinking about engaging with the methodologies. And thus interventionists need to understand, and be able to identify, when leaders are being driven by the need to create a plausible good story rather than a factually accurate timeline of events. Attributions will be made that can be flawed and hinder genuine paradigm or mindset shift and so the use of reflexive practice is one way to challenge stories that are diverging in an unhelpful way. Another is to recognize that events will be embellished and rearranged in time in order to create better drama as happened with the ah-ha! moments and once again reflexive practice can create a more accurate story of how and when ah-ha! moments will be used as part of our sensemaking.

References

Bellinger, G. 2017. Really? Whoa!. https://www.linkedin.com/pulse/really-whoa-gene-bellinger [Online]. [Accessed 17th Feb 2017 2017].

Boje, D. M. 1991. The storytelling organization: A study of story performance in and office-supply firm. *Administrative Science Quarterly*, Vol. 36, 106–126.

Gabriel, Y. 2000. *Storytelling in Organizations: Facts, Fictions, and Fantasies*, Oxford, Oxford University Press.

Garfinkel, H. 1967. *Studies in Ethnomethodology*, Englewood Cliffs, Prentice Hall.

Gladwell, M. 2000. *The Tipping Point: How Little Things Can Make a Big Difference*, Boston, Little Brown.

Goldratt, E. M. & Cox, J. 1984. *The Goal: A Process of Ongoing Improvement*, Great Barrington, The North River Press Publishing Corporation.

Johnson, S. 1998. *Who Moved My Cheese?: An Amazing Way to Deal with Change in Your Work and in Your Life*, New York, G. P. Putnam's and Sons.

Kets De Vries, M. F. R. 2015. *Telling Fairy Tales in the Boardroom: How to Make Sure Your Organization Lives Happily Ever After*, London, Palgrave MacMillan.

Lundin, S. C., Paul, H. & Christensen, J. 2000. *Fish!: A Remarkable Way to Boost Morale and Improve Results*, London, Hodder & Stoughton.

Merriam-Webster. 2017. *Epiphany* [Online]. Merriam-Webster: Merriam-Webster.com. [Accessed 4th Feb. 2017].
OED. 2015. *Oxford English Dictionary - Online* [Online]. OED. Available: http://www.oed.com/view/Entry/190981?rskey=NQUaEe&result=1#eid [Accessed 25th January 2015].
Weick, K. E. 1995. *Sensemaking in Organizations*, London, Sage Publications.

6 Displacement of Concepts

Paradigm Shift or Paradigm Expansion?

Displacement of concepts is something that we all experience. It is an important element of sensemaking which can greatly help with adoption of new ways of thinking but is often misunderstood or overlooked by interventionists.

I was discussing my postmodern perspective on organizing and leading with a leader and he challenged me that there seemed to be a paradox in what I was saying. He suggested that postmodernism deconstructs modernist thinking about organization and leaders, but here I was working with leaders in modernist creations called organizations. Without being rude, he asked was I not being a hypocrite? What, he asked, was new about my approach and was it not essentially still a modernist ontology? There did appear to be a contradiction in claiming a postmodern ontology while working within the modernist concept of organizations, especially when one considers the postmodern belief that they are nothing more than socially co-created concepts used to create the illusion of stability in an environment of constant flux and change.

My colleague and I spent a long time debating the apparent paradox and it so happened that the discussion took place in the Victoria and Albert museum in London where we had been holding a meeting. It was at this point I spotted something which helped crystallize my thinking and which I have since used many times with leaders to help their sensemaking of moving to a different mindset. I invite you to try the exercise now ... I would like you to think of some words that capture the key features of a 'dish'.

Leaders usually come up with features such as container, sides, base, different shapes, and so forth. What I saw in the Victoria and Albert Museum in London was a Postmodern Corral Dish by Richard Slee with an accompanying narrative that states that its postmodern design 'upset traditional assumptions about the object's use, form and subject matter' (you can see a picture of the dish on the V&A website). It has no base and an open side and is a dish for things that need held in one place but do not need contained. It is a dish that corrals things without containing them and so would be useful for things like fruit but useless for liquids.

Like most leaders, my concept of a dish had always been of containing but now my conceptualization had been extended to include corralling and this reconceptualization aligns with Schon's (1963) theorization of the displacement of concepts. My original concept of a dish remained but had now been displaced and extended to include a new element of corralling. We all experienced similar displacement of concepts as children when our concept of water as a liquid was displaced to include water as a solid when we first encountered ice and then water as a gas when to our amazement we learned that clouds were made up of water. We still had a concept of water, but it had been reconceptualized to include it's three different states.

It seemed to me that this served as a useful way of addressing the apparent paradox of a postmodern approach to changing modernist organizations. Our discussion about the Corral Dish helped me reconcile the inherent paradox of postmodernism which seeks to challenge the truth and reality of what we know, and even the ideas of *true* and *know*. The Corral Dish offers a useful analogy for a postmodern reconceptualization of organizations. As Chia argues, the modernist concept of organization may be intrinsically opposed to change but that does not mean he is arguing against the need for a concept of organization, nor the omnipresence of change. He points out that:

> ... organization and order represents the cumulative productive efforts of human intervention to temporarily stave off the nomadic and immanent forces of change. Contrary to the commonly held view, order and organization do not reflect the law of things but their exception. They are the outcome of an existential 'Will to Order'. **Without organization and the stability and regularity it forges, and hence the predictability it earns, human life would be chaotic and eminently unliveable.** (my emphasis)
>
> (Chia, 2003, p.134)

So, postmodernist thought challenges traditional assumptions about organizational purpose, design and principles and seeks to reconceptualize it, as Chia puts it, as a will to order rather than an existing state of order.

From this perspective there is no paradox in adopting a postmodern change methodology to work with leaders in modernist organizations – my role as internal consultant was to seek to engage leaders by questioning their current concept of organization and challenging their current thinking about purpose, design and principles of organization. I was trying to help leaders make sense of a move from a modernist force of opposition to change to a postmodern acceptance of change in which the conceptualization of leadership is more akin to the quote frequently attributed to Otto Von Bismarck[1]:

> Man cannot control the current of events, he can only float with them and steer

A postmodern leadership ontology does not remove the need for organization but it does require a very different concept of both organizing and leading.

However, some academics argue that displacement of concepts can only happen within, not between, paradigms and so would not resolve my conflict of using a postmodern perspective in modernist organizations. Guba and Lincoln (2005) criticize positivists who argue that the scientific paradigms are commensurable and can be 'retrofitted to each other in ways that make the simultaneous practice of both possible' (p.200). Fabian (2000) summarizes the distinctive nature of subjectivist research by arguing that:

> ... theorists from different paradigms may claim to study "organizations" through "scientific methods" but disagree about what an organization entails (ontology) or about the process of scientific enquiry (epistemology). For instance, a subjectivist theorist might assume (in contrast to an economist) that there are no "objective" organizational boundaries – just preferences for action arising from the social and symbolic constructions of individuals
>
> (p.351)

This line of reasoning implies that sensemaking embraces a paradigmatic 'either/or' approach. Certainly many change methodologies, modern and postmodern, use the language of change *from* old *to* new thinking and the leader sensemaking stories in Chapter 3 contained tales of a move from old world to new world thinking and a crossing of the Rubicon with no return to the old ways of thinking. However, my research found that leader sensemaking frequently embraces an 'and' approach which includes displacement of concepts even at paradigm level much like my own sensemaking of the paradox of a postmodern heretic working in modernist organizations.

One example of displacement of concepts which seemed to involve an element of combined paradigms came from TL, a Director of OD&HR who explained to a staff conference what the implications of the transformation methodology were for his internal support function:

TL: In a traditional sense when we look at re-organization, what senior people like me do is get a flip chart out and draw lots of boxes and allocate people to functions without really knowing what's going on in the organization. One of the things we do around this [transformation] approach is to let the structure form itself and continue to re-form as circumstances change. It's a challenge for us

> because we're used to stability and continuity but the reality is our environment is constantly changing so we need to be nimble and agile enough to adapt our structures and roles as fast as the environment changes.

TL seemed to be combining a postmodern perspective of organizing rather than organization, but at the same time retaining the concepts of organizational structures and roles. He was recognizing that the modernist step of refreezing changes to organizational structures and processes simply embeds changes that, because of the continuous flux that is the environment, would quickly be out of date and inappropriate. His response to this was to invert traditional thinking and instead of creating fixed structures and roles instead let them emerge from the activity of organizing. In other words his concepts of organization and structure as nouns have been displaced and reconceptualized as organizing and structuring as verbs.

I asked TL what he thought the practical implications were for leader thinking:

TL: Good question! Leaders are used to fixed structures and traditional hierarchies. We've [OD and HR function] been guilty of reinforcing ... or maybe we're even the main culprit, in silo structures and hierarchy culture so now I've got to try and get leaders to think differently about what they really need. I had a session with the Directors from two directorates about the structure of a jointly funded operation, so they were both describing the same thing. The first is old fashioned command and control but the second has used systems thinking for a couple of years now and is a solid systems thinker. I asked them to draw the high-level structure on a flipchart and you could see clearly the difference in thinking. The first one drew a bog-standard rigid silo and hierarchy but the second one drew a more shapeless, organic and fluid picture. How they think about it will determine what it becomes and how it's led and it's a good example of the implications of this stuff.

I have worked with many leaders that have engaged with the same methodology that TL was referring to. It uses the concept of a paradigm shift from 'command and control' thinking to 'systems thinking'. Leaders who are advocates of the methodology tend to tell sensemaking stories similar to those in Chapter 3 which entail some sort of road to Damascus conversion from old world command and control modernist thinking to new world postmodern systems thinking. However, my own interpretation is that all is not quite as it seems and there is actually a strong element of displacement of concepts within these stories. I have used this particular methodology on many occasions and observed what appears to be a paradox that is best understood by the sensemaking element of compresence of opposites (which I cover in Chapter 11). Leaders sensemaking reality is that they have a new paradigm of organizing and leading, but at the same time their new thinking includes displaced concepts of organizing and leading as demonstrated by BL, a senior leader in a Global manufacturing and sales organization and which reminded me of my postmodern dish experience:

BL: Ron, I think the problem with the methodology is that it has this you're one or the other mentality. So you're either a command and control leader or you're a systems thinking leader. Well I'm a systems thinking leader through and through but I also like to be in control. I mean it could be just a language thing, but you and I know that in command and control thinking the control is just an illusion whereas in system thinking you get more control by giving it up (laughs) ... but really you get more control of outcomes by not trying to micromanage inputs if you know what I mean. But it's not just that ... I think that the either/or thing is wrong too because there are times when you have to be command and control because circumstances demand it. I mean you're a systems thinker but you were full-on command and control when you had to lead the product recall so you probably know what I mean yeah?

BL is saying that he has embraced the new way of thinking but that does not mean giving up all aspects of the old way of thinking. Just as with my paradox of being a postmodernist in the modernist world of organizations, so BL is a postmodernist operating in a world of command and control thinking. Whereas the methodology talked of moving from command and control to systems thinking, BL had reconceptualized his concept of leadership which now included command and control *and* systems thinking. Systems thinking was his new orthodoxy but that did not rule out using command and control when circumstances merited it, just as I might corral fruit in my postmodern dish but return to a modernist dish for soup. BL correctly assumed I shared his sensemaking because of my experience leading a product recall when I was Operations Director. Like BL, I was a confirmed systems thinker but shared his unease about the idea that this involved a total rejection of command and control thinking. When I was told that one of our products had a fault that involved risk to life I reverted to 'old world' command and control thinking – this was a crisis that required immediate directive action, something that I would have normally rejected as the wrong thing to do but which in this case was necessary. I witnessed leaders in similar positions during my research and in some cases the outcome was that once back in old world they firmly stayed there despite the 'crisis' having passed, thus suggesting that their crossing of the Rubicon to new world thinking was anything but a one way journey. In other cases the leaders only used command and control thinking until the crisis was past and then quickly returned to systems thinking, thus suggesting that their crossing of the Rubicon may not have been one way but when they did cross back to old world thinking it was very much a temporary return.

Another example of what felt like displaced concepts arose when I spoke to a RD, a leader in a global organization known for having rejected modernist thinking about organizations. I told RD how impressed I was by the concept of no hierarchy, no job roles, lattice structure in which everyone is an associate and no leaders. Instead they focused on organizing in response to change and leading by letting people with appropriate skills and credibility emerge from within teams. RD listened politely to me telling him how his company organized themselves then said to me:

RD: hmm well I guess you are about 90% right (laughs). Most people think the same as you because that's what they've read about us. And for the most part it's right but it's not quite the nirvana you've described. In some ways it's a bit Animal Farm – all associates are equal but some are a bit more equal than others. We're all associates but only some associates can fly first class ... and I'm not one of them! (laughs). There's no hierarchy but only a few associates can make strategic decisions that others can't. I mean don't get me wrong, we are very very different from the way most companies organize ... but we've not completely lost some of the traditional stuff ... just rebadged it as something else. The stuff about no roles is right but we still have people who are specialists and the no roles stuff is more about just making sure we pull together the right people with the right skills onto a team.

Leader sensemaking is complex and paradoxical. The other eight elements all strengthen and weaken commitment to existing *and* new paradigms and mindsets but at the same time leaders create sensemaking stories of a move from/to. Those same leaders whose stories reflect a one-way journey do not, however, completely discard their modernist concepts of organization, leadership and change. Like the stories of the leaders in Chapter 3, my own sensemaking began with an *or* perspective. Leaders are modernist *or* postmodern in perspective. But my sensemaking developed to a point where I believe change agents need to accept that there is an *and* in which modernism and postmodernism overlap. Leaders can be a bit of both in other words. Such a view may appear heretical to both modernists and postmodernists alike, but I believe the displacement of concepts has demonstrated that old and new concepts co-exist at paradigmatic level. If leaders engage with postmodern influenced methodologies they will experience a displacement of their concepts, which embraces both paradigms, but paradoxically their post-engagement sensemaking stories are likely to be of crossing the Rubicon into a new world of thinking in which there is no turning back, in other words they will sensemake old *or* new world. This can become a self-sustaining sensemaking loop as leaders give others preunderstanding that they will experience a one-way journey from 'old' paradigm to 'new'. They are giving others an interpretation of what they will experience and the danger is that this is exactly how leaders will retrospectively sensemake their stories (I discuss this issue further in Chapter 12). The challenge for postmodern influenced methodologies and interventionists is to recognize that paradigm shift is not about clear distinctions between one or another, it is much more likely to entail a displacement of concepts that fuses both paradigms. Concepts are reconceptualized such that they embrace elements of both paradigms.

Note

1 This quote is widely attributed to Bismarck but despite searching I can find no source that confirms where or when he made it.

References

Chia, R. 2003. Organization theory as a postmodern science. *In:* Tsoukas, H. & Knudsen, C. (eds.) *The Oxford Handbook of Organization Theory: Meta-Theoretical Perspectives.* (pp. 113–142). Oxford: Oxford University Press.

Fabian, F. H. 2000. Keeping the tension: Pressures to keep the controversy in the management discipline. *The Academy of Management Review*, Vol. 25, 350–371.

Guba, E. G. & Lincoln, Y. S. 2005. Paradigmatic controversies, contradictions, and emerging confluences. *In:* Denzin, N. K. & Lincoln, Y. S. (eds.) *The Sage Handbook of Qualitative Research.* 3rd ed. (pp. 191–215). Oakland: Sage.

Schon, D. A. 1963. *Displacement of Concepts*, London, Tavistock Publications.

7 Preunderstanding

A Little (or a Lot of) Knowledge Can Be a Dangerous Thing

At the start of this book I asked you if you believed Earth to be flat or round and whether it revolved around the sun or the other way round. My question now is 'how do you know?'

It is worth thinking about this for a while because our sensemaking of anything is profoundly affected by what we currently believe to be 'true'. I believe the Earth to be round and that it revolves around the sun. I know this from being taught at school, from watching science programs on television, from films and books, from listening to other people, from websites and pictures and from many other sources that I can't even actively recall. My beliefs that the Earth is round and that it revolves around the sun, together with the multiple sources from which I formed these beliefs are what can be termed my preunderstanding. You will similarly have preunderstanding that in any situation will answer the question 'how do you know?'

No leader in an organization is a completely blank slate, we all have experiences and perceptions which we bring with us, which form our preunderstanding and which significantly impact how we make sense of new experiences. This is not to say that our preunderstanding is a bad thing – it can enrich and inform our understanding but interventionists have to be aware of the challenges that it can present.

Gummesson (2000) explains that there are two sources of preunderstanding - first-hand direct personal experience and the second-hand experience of others. All the sources of my knowledge about the Earth being round came from others – my parents, teachers, family, friends, writers, broadcasters and so on. I have no direct personal experience that the Earth is round. For example, I have not traveled into space and seen it with my own eyes. The nearest thing to personal experience that I had was on long haul flights around the globe when I was told that if I looked out the window of the plane I would notice the curve in the horizon, which would have been first-hand evidence that the Earth is round. I strained my eyes looking for it, but I have to be honest and say the horizon always looked flat to me. Nevertheless, notwithstanding my lack of personal experience, I choose the weight of second-hand experience of others and believe that the Earth is round.

All the leaders in the research organizations I worked with brought their many years of preunderstanding to the setting, and most of it was second-hand experience, with most, for example, having attended management training courses and having undertaken business and management qualifications. Seddon argues that this academic preunderstanding has a major impact and that 'leadership ends up being what the various theorists postulate it to be.' (Seddon, 2003, p. 105) and in Chapter 3 I gave examples of leaders using their academic preunderstanding in their sensemaking stories. Sensemaking involves plausibility, and the leaders used their extensive discussions about their second-hand preunderstanding to give a plausible explanation of their flawed old world thinking and thus setting the scene for their dramatic move to new world thinking. They talked about their formal management education and many spoke of the books and writings on leadership which had shaped their beliefs.

The leaders I worked with in the research organizations brought three categories of preunderstanding to bear on my attempts to get them to engage with the methodologies I was using:

- A small number of leaders who had no preunderstanding of the methodology
- The majority of leaders who had second-hand preunderstanding, most often from hearing about the methodologies from colleagues
- A small number of leaders who had first-hand personal experience of engaging with the methodologies

No Preunderstanding of the Methodology

Imagine I point to something unfamiliar and ask you what it is. You will look at the object and then compare it with your memories of similar looking objects until either you get a good enough match to say 'it's a ...' or you just cannot make a close enough match and you have to say 'I don't know what it is', although our bias is towards making sense of situations and things and so we strive to find something to match it to, however tenuous. Thus, when we encounter objects or concepts our natural response is to use our preunderstanding and go through a process of 'it looks/smells/feels/tastes/sounds like...' The risk of this searching of past understanding is that it is not always accurate.

It should be no surprise therefore that leaders similarly use their preunderstanding to make sense of novel situations. A small number of leaders I worked with said they had no knowledge of the methodology I was going to be using at all. They demonstrated the initial sensemaking response of listening to my overview of the methodology and matching it to their organizational preunderstanding. In summary their sense was that it looks/sounds like change projects we've done before and therefore should be managed in the same way:

WD: So I keep saying this, it's got to be within a program management approach … that we put some milestones and deadlines, etc. I talked about us meeting this afternoon and starting to schedule out how we are going to work as a small team, at least over the next sort of eight to ten weeks, and I suggest that's enough time to aim to come back with, you know, a clear update about where we got to and whether we think we can deliver redesign and savings.

I had spent some time with this small group of leaders explaining the mindset changes that the transformation methodology would entail and in particular its rejection of targets, deadlines and detailed outcomes. But the methodology was still an unknown to them and so they searched for 'looks like' preunderstanding to match it to. WD was making clear that she had had decided that the methodology was a change project to be managed in a traditional project management environment. Within the group of leaders there was a mixture of acceptance that it needed to be project managed but also some acceptance that doing so contained inherent risks:

WD: But this is where I get very very concerned about the role the Program Board play, because the scope, to some extent, has to be owned by the Program Board, I think. You know, they have to be clear about what they're trying to … what the scale … you know, what is the problem? What's in that problem and what areas they're looking at?

TL: The tricky but the interesting thing for me then, variously expressed round the table, is that individually and collectively some leaders haven't engaged with the approach and therefore they could quickly become a hindrance as distinct from an enabler. Now when we move into grand design, redesign, what we're going to do is hold [them] to account for the decisions that we can't, we don't have authority to exercise, and that's going to shine a big light on how they individually and collectively think, which is where I think somewhere in our design we need to think about how we drag them in … so that they understand that this actually is their fault and worth spending some time on paying some attention to and actually coughing some resource up to enable it to happen.

WD: I am absolutely aware that we've got to have a program approach to this so that if we have got milestones where decisions are made and timescales are put in place to deliver … if it's not delivered we challenge the Program Board to why, you know, because if they become the problem, we've got to highlight that they're the problem and that we're not, they're not taking appropriate action.

The social sensemaking starts with WD surfacing her preunderstanding of program boards which is that they often lack or lose focus and clarity about what the 'project' is trying to achieve. TL agrees and voices the concern of others in the group that the wider group of leaders 'haven't engaged with the approach' and could become an obstacle to mindset change rather than engaging in it. TL and the others clearly felt some unease about the use of a project management approach, but nevertheless the group sensemaking at this point was single loop learning using tried and tested methods from their preunderstanding.

Second-Hand Preunderstanding

Most of the leaders I worked with had preunderstanding gained from talking to colleagues who had their own second-hand experience, and in a few cases first-hand experience, of the methodologies I was using. In one of the global organizations I worked in, I was one of a small team of internal consultants introducing the methodology at different times in different areas of the business. Leaders in the organization regularly attended global leadership events and most had spoken to other leaders who had engaged with the methodology. I asked them to work in small groups and answer the following questions about what they had heard of the methodology:

- How does it happen?
- How does it feel to engage with it?
- How long does it take?

I wanted their collective sense of these issues and I have aggregated the three group responses as there were no significant differences in their feedback:

- How does it happen?
    - It's reactive
    - It's a long-term culture change program
    - It's top down but involves everyone
- How does it feel to engage with it?
    - It's a bumpy road to success
    - It feels like more work
    - Honest feedback is interpreted as resistance
    - People are not happy with the status quo and want change
- How long does it take?
    - Too long! Never stops
    - It feels rushed
    - It involves endless churn
    - Change is constant/continuous (and that's good)

I wondered if some elements of the feedback reflected specific preunderstanding of the methodology or more general preunderstanding of organizational change in general, so I asked the four groups if this was the case:

Leader 1: we talked about people we'd known that had done [methodology] and some of the stuff we'd heard from them. But it's hard to separate what they told us with what happens generally because we've been round this circle so many times. I'm sure you'll explain the difference of [methodology] from the other corporate [change] projects we've been through in the last few years.

Leader 2: we said it was reactive because that's the only way [organization name] does change. I've heard that [methodology] is sent in to sort out 'problem' areas in the eyes of Group.

Leader 3: we were told it's a long-term change program. Group have decided we've got to do it so it's like others and a bit top down. But leaders that have done it also say it's very liberating and are very passionate about it so we're interested to see why they are so passionate.

Me: ok thanks. Can I just pick up on one other thing? There's [sic] some contradictions in the feedback, so for instance group 1 you fedback that it's too long and never stops but also that it's rushed! (laughter). I'm just trying to understand what your thinking was there?

Leader 1: it may look like we are being inconsistent (laughs) but we're just reflecting what we've heard that there's a push to do things quickly but it seems to take an awful long time for some of the interventions that we've heard of. I guess we thought we'd stick 'em down coz we don't know which is true (laughs).

Their feedback seems to have been influenced by their largely negative preunderstanding of the current approach to change and at this point they could not sense how the methodology would be any different. But their feedback also reflected things that they had heard from other leaders who had engaged with the methodology and this may account for the compresence of opposites (this element of sensemaking is covered in Chapter 11) such as believing that the methodology is both a long-term culture change program and a reactive fix, or that the methodology is top down but involves everyone or that it can be both rushed and too long. While some of these opposites were differences in what individuals had heard from colleagues, it was also clear that the leaders sensemaking was beginning to embrace that perhaps the methodology could involve both realities. I had anticipated that some of these preunderstandings might exist and wanted to create some alternative preunderstandings for the leaders. Notwithstanding that getting the leaders commitment compliance depended on my own credibility as an 'expert' I had decided that with a larger group like this that it might be better to invite some leaders who had previously engaged with the methodology to give their sense of what it was like. This was not a scripted or manufactured input and instead I asked the two invited leaders to comment on the feedback from the groups. The discussion was wide ranging and strayed into business issues not directly related to leader engagement with the methodology and so I have extracted some key points that I feel reflect the preunderstanding that my invited guests gave to the leaders:

SP: well it's interesting to hear what you've heard and I recognize some of it but some of it seems way off to be honest. I know that there's a feeling that [methodology] takes forever and I must admit that's what I thought when I was first asked if I wanted to do it. Not got the time for all that navel gazing stuff and so on. And to be honest it did actually feel a bit like that to begin with. One of the team members said it felt like wading through treacle and we kind of wondered when is this ever going to end. But then we could start to see the picture we were building and it started to get exciting and we were in a rush to start fixing things and actually Ron had to kind of put the brakes on us and slow us down (laughs). So actually we did amazing things much much faster than we'd ever do it in old world but yeah at times it felt kind of slow.

I'm not sure who told you it was top down but actually it's quite the opposite. Of course you as leaders have to own it and create the environment that allows it to happen but it ain't going to work if you just tell people what's going to happen. The great thing about it from my perspective is that it let me engage everyone in my business and they just took it and ran. All I had to do was support them and give them the belief I would act on what we found.

GJ: yeah absolutely I agree about the energy that you get when you really empower your people to use [methodology]. In my old world I was used to telling them what to do and I would have felt like a weak leader if I let them tell me what to do but that's almost where you get to. The thing that really blows your mind is when you suddenly realize that you can be a much better and stronger leader by just actually letting go and not trying to control so much. Seems a bit counter-intuitive but it's true.

Me: but did it feel like it was being done top-down to you when you first got involved?

GJ: oh I see.. no I don't think so. I remember being asked if I was up for doing it and I knew if I said no there'd have probably been something else imposed on us but I was willing to have a go and see if it would work in my area. It was obvious my boss or someone above her wanted me to try it but it was more of seeing whether it was something that would work in our business and if not then do something else.

SP: I think the other thing worth mentioning is your stuff [leader feedback] about it's never ending. Well yeah that's kind of the whole point of it – it's about us thinking differently and always questioning why we do things. So what I didn't really get at the start is that it's not a project that you finish, dust your hands and walk away saying 'job well done'. Once you finish the first cycle you move straight on to doing it again ... it's a bit of a Forth Bridge job – once you get to one end and finish you start at the beginning again.

GJ: I think the point about a bumpy ride is true ... no point in looking at it through rose tinted glasses. It will challenge how you think about leading and some of the stuff you uncover will be really uncomfortable. On top of that you'll be up against a lot of systems conditions that it's your job to go out and change which won't be easy. So it'll be a challenge but you won't look back.

I felt that my guest leaders had credibility with the leaders and had addressed most of the concerns that they had. They had proved helpful in creating some new preunderstanding even if the leaders still did not fully understand the methodology. SP and GJ had also established credibility with their honesty and not using 'rose tinted glasses'. They acknowledged the difficulties leaders can expect, which was another example of preunderstanding that should help leaders as they sensemake during the 'wading through treacle' times. I asked the leaders if what they had heard had given them a different sense of the methodology:

- It's helpful to hear from people who've done it and understand why the people we had spoken to had such mixed messages
- Well it's exciting and daunting in equal measures because GJ has been very honest about the bumpy ride we're in for
- Hmmm ... I get the positive vibes and I do feel a bit better that it's not going to be the same as all the others, but I do wonder if the senior leaders are really up for the changes we come up with.
- The energy thing has come over clearly and I was the one who said people are fed up with the status quo so I definitely think we can tap into that desire for change. But I don't want to create false hope for staff ... if we get them all excited about helping us redesign the

business and then we're told can't do it, it'd be worse than doing nothing.

- I'm not trying to be negative and I'm sure it's a great approach. But I do worry about the time and resources that we'll be asked to put into this. We've got to keep the business running and I don't see how we can pull a bunch of people out the work and still do that.

There was a consensus that the methodology potentially offered positive benefits for the leaders and their language suggested that the new pre-understanding had moved them a bit closer to commitment compliance (see Chapter 9). The phrases 'we come up with', 'if we get them all excited' and 'the bumpy ride we're in for' imply that these leaders sensemaking has led them to accepting they will engage with the methodology. Other leaders were less clear about their commitment at this stage and were still expressing concerns, not about the methodology but about the theories-in-action of senior leaders and the difficulties of committing resources.

Personal Experience of Engaging with the Methodology

A small number of leaders I worked with had actually engaged with the methodology several years previously. I was a little surprised to learn this because if the methodology was successful surely they would now be telling similar sensemaking stories to the leaders in Chapter 3 and would not be needing my support to engage with it again. So I suspected their experience had not been good and that therefore their preunderstanding of the methodology would be negative, and this indeed proved to be the case:

MH: I've got a lot of experience of [methodology] and it's not good. We tried it three years back and it was painful ... I had a team of people taken out my business for six months just to do an understand of 'as is' and got nothing out of it. I got a presentation that had a load of data and didn't tell me anything. They spent two weeks just trying to come up with purpose! I've been told we've got to do [methodology] again but I can tell you that if you're suggesting I've got to pull a load of staff out to do all that again it's not on. I'm struggling to run the business as it is and taking a bunch of staff out to spend six months producing nothing isn't an option.

Me: oh I see. Who helped you with the methodology at that time?

MH: it was a consultant the company brought in ... didn't seem to have a clue what was happening.

The leader's short explanation contained a number of elements which my own sensemaking was trying to synthesize:

- Was the leader exaggerating – did it really take six months or just feel like it took six months?
- If it really took six months how on earth could that be?
- This feels an awful lot like a leader who last time round saw the methodology as project to be delegated to a team, waited six months for feedback, then felt that the data told him nothing.
- The leader appeared to be challenging me to say that we would be doing the same again, so that he could refuse to engage on the grounds it didn't work last time.

I had no reason to doubt his statement regarding the six months, and it was indeed subsequently borne out by other members of his team. But even if he was unconsciously exaggerating, it was his current reality and challenging it when I had no evidence otherwise would have simply embedded his negative view of 'consultants'. However, I was struggling to make sense of this timescale because I couldn't understand how this could be. My own preunderstanding from experience in similar sized business areas was that it should take no more than six weeks for the data gathering exercise and I could not understand how it could take six months. The leader said that the consultant didn't know what he was doing but I wondered if perhaps he knew exactly what he was doing. For an external consultant paid on a daily rate, six months chargeable work is better than six weeks chargeable work. However, this was speculation on my part. Nevertheless, and notwithstanding that I had no evidence other than what the leader had told me, my sensemaking was that perhaps the leader had, based on his direct personal experience, reason to be suspicious of the methodology and its value. I would have to give him a sense that working with me would be different and that I would have to give him a sense that there was a reason he got nothing out the last intervention and that working with me would be different.

Finally, I felt that leader was currently in a position of forced compliance. He had been told by his own leader that he 'had' to engage with the methodology and so there was no choice. It seemed to me that he was looking for a way to challenge his forced compliance and creating a stand-off with me was a way to create choice. He had evidence that the methodology didn't work the last time and all he needed to hear me say was that we would be repeating the steps that happened last time and this would be sufficient for him to push back against his forced compliance. It was clear that I would have to give him a sense that I could offer him something different, and positive, if he worked with me.

The brief outline MH gave me of his preunderstanding and the sense I made of it led me to try to counter his perception of the methodology and create some positive preunderstanding that would move him from a feeling of being forced to engage, to commitment compliance. I decided I wanted to address the issues he had surfaced but also create the sense that there are myths about the methodology and give some general examples to attempt to dispel the myths.

Me: I'm not surprised you describe it as painful ... I'm shocked to be honest. I've worked with leaders from many different organizations all around the world in all sizes of organization, some much bigger than this, and I've ***never*** seen a data gathering phase that lasted six months. I'm confident that in your business it would be completed in less than six weeks. Two weeks to define a customer purpose is astonishing ... the last intervention I did, agreeing customer purpose took 15 minutes. I mean I know there's still pain from taking people out the work to do data gathering no matter how short the time but my role is to make sure you can keep the business running whilst we work to minimize any disruption. And I think the only other thing I'd say is that I'm certainly not going to waste time help you gathering data that doesn't help you find new ways of designing the business. I'm paid to make sure you get pace AND help you get value as well – else I'll be looking for another job (laughs).

MH: 15 mins!! Wow ok. Well that's certainly much more realistic. Six weeks rather than six months is a lot better too but I'd need to be sure it's not going to end up like six months the last time. I know it's three years [ago] but am I really going to get anything substantially different from the information I got back then? I know there's been some changes since then but I've got a pretty good handle on what they've been.

Me: Well if there's a chance to use previous data that would make sense but three years is actually a long time in business and at the very least we'd need to validate any data we use which would mean doing some degree of rechecking. But, like I say, I've ***never*** been on an intervention that took six months to do that type of data gathering. How long it takes is up to you and the priority you give it but with the right resources and leadership by you it will definitely be done within six weeks maybe even less. The key is to surface insights that you wouldn't have the chance or time to get otherwise. Of course you've got a good handle on your business and this is certainly ***not*** an exercise in telling you that you don't know how to run it. For me the key is to let you get insights that help you achieve the strategic challenges you've been set. Unlike the consultant three years ago I wouldn't be doing it for you – I'd be helping you understand how to use the methodology. You own it and you decide what you get out of it.

MH: actually Ron that's quite reassuring to hear. I'm not saying I'm happy to be doing it (laughs) but you seem to understand what the business needs better. We still need to sort out the resource commitments. Funny you should say that it's not about telling me how bad I'm running the business because I know other leaders that felt that's exactly what they were being told.

Me: I've been an operations director in organizations and I sure as hell wouldn't take well to someone telling me I didn't know how to run my business! (laughs)

MH: (laughs) ok at least we understand each other. But I'll be honest ... I'm not convinced yet.. I'm in the shop but I'm not buying yet (laughs).

Me: how's about I give you a buy one get one free offer?

Both: (laughs)

MH was surprised at the alternative possibility that the methodology could be much faster than his previous experience of it. My 15 minutes and six weeks preunderstanding examples seemed sufficiently dramatic but credible enough to go some way towards countering his existing preunderstanding of the methodology as a very slow and cumbersome experience. His expressions of 'wow ok', 'much more realistic', and 'that's quite reassuring' suggest that he is sensemaking that the methodology could have different outcomes to those he has experienced. I had been concerned that his preunderstanding meant he was looking for an excuse to get out of the forced compliance situation he was in but my attempts to give him an alternative understanding of what the methodology could be like gave him a different sense of what he was being asked to commit to. MH was still cautious and had concerns that I would need to overcome, but I feel that establishing his preunderstanding and creating alternative options opened the door for me to negotiate commitment compliance based on my credibility as an expert, rather than forced compliance based on being told he must engage by his own leader.

MH's personal experience led to a negative view of the methodology in its entirety. The other leader I encountered who had personal experience had a different negative experience. JT was a leader in the public sector organization and in my first meeting I asked him about his preunderstanding:

Me: Can I just check what you know about the methodology? I like to understand any knowledge leaders have before we start so that I can adjust what we do accordingly. By the way, I think you know about my research yeah? [JT nods] so I'm always checking leaders awareness before we start working together. Usually they have some but I don't want to make any assumptions.

JT: Well I've actually done [methodology] before. I worked in [named organization – public sector housing organization] and we did it in our repairs function.

Me: oh I see, I'm sorry, I didn't know that ... I'm glad I asked then (laughs). How did it go?

JT: I'd like to say it was good (laughs).

Me: it sounds like there's a 'but' coming (laughs).

JT: Hmm there is really. We.. you know what it's like.. we identified all sorts of crap during data gathering and it was obvious there was a lot we could do to improve things. So we got stuck in and made a lot of improvements but the big things ... you know, the big systems conditions ... there was no appetite to tackle them and that was the problem. At the end of the day all the good work we did just got unraveled and politicians and the other senior leaders just drove the crap back in. So to be honest it felt like 'why bother?'. You just make a lot of enemies and piss everyone off. We delivered some great results but it wasn't sustainable and as far as I know it's as bad as ever if not worse. So got to say I'm not sure I'm looking forward to reliving that experience.

Unlike MH, JT's personal experience of the methodology was positive in the sense of the insights he gained and the opportunity it presented. His negative perception was on the sustainability of the change in thinking when other leaders in the business still hold a modernist perspective. When he says there was no appetite to tackle the systems conditions (which are the manifestations of current leader mindsets) it suggests that his thinking had changed, but he was faced with the 'ignorant others' identified in the leader stories in Chapter 3. I wanted to explore this further before deciding what alternative preunderstanding examples I wanted to try and present:

Me: that sounds so frustrating and I can understand why you wouldn't want a repeat of it. Can I just check my understanding with you ... you didn't have a problem with the methodology and you could see the thinking that needed to change ... but the problem was senior leaders and politicians in the Council didn't?

JT: yeah that's pretty much it.

Me: ok but given the improvements you made and the potential for more why do you think they didn't buy in?

JT: Simple really ... they felt we were attacking their little empires and there was no way they were going to let that happen. So it was kind of just get on with improving your repairs and stop trying to run the rest of the council. They didn't get that they were causing most the problems and so we couldn't do what we wanted. The politicians and their targets and silo thinking drove the old ways straight back in to repairs. [the methodology] can give you a different perspective but it's also career limiting if no one else changes their perspective! (laughs).

My sense of JT's comments was that he had experienced the opportunity to view reality through a new lens and had questioned his existing mindset. But when he talked about the forces of inertia in the form of politicians and other senior leaders, he seemed to be describing Lewin's forces of opposition in his force field analysis. The modernist ontological perspective is widespread and deeply embedded in leader mindsets (Chia, 1994, 1995, 1996, 1997, 1999, 2003, Chia and Holt, 2006, Deming, 1982, 1994, Seddon, 2003, 2008, 2010, Senge, 1990, 1992, Senge et al., 1999). Any methodology that seeks to change this mindset therefore faces significant forces of opposition which will pull any change in mindset back to the current status quo. JT seemed to me to be describing just such an experience and this has left him with a negative experience of sticking his head above the mindset change parapet and suffering the consequences. My sense was that if I wanted to get his commitment compliance for a second attempt at engaging with the methodology the preunderstanding that I would need to create was different from the approach I used with MT. JT was already convinced of the potential value of the methodology and what he needed was reassurance about was the ability to get wider senior leadership engagement and the longer term sustainability of the methodology if he worked with me:

Me: Your experience isn't unique but I can say from my own experience that it's not the norm either. I think getting others convinced is the biggest challenge of the methodology but you know for yourself that the methodology works. So there's an opportunity here to avoid what happened in the last organization and there are opportunities in [name of organization] to take a different approach that focuses on getting senior leaders engaged. I've supported leaders who not only got their own leadership teams to change their thinking but even got legislation changes that everyone else said would be impossible.

JT: changed legislation? [I gave detail of the example]. Right, well fair enough. I'm not wanting a repeat of what happened last time so what's your thinking about where our senior team is on this?

Me: I've spoken with them and you know how it is – they don't know what they don't know about a different way of thinking. But I've sounded out their willingness to question some of the fundamentals about how we organize and run this business. I got a sense that as long as we keep them engaged throughout so that nothing comes as a shock, they'll be up for it. In my experience the problem comes when we present data and systems conditions as a fait acompli at the end of data gathering and they feel they're being attacked, blamed or boxed into a corner. I know because I've made that mistake myself and had the same experience you did. But if we work together to manage their engagement, I think you could find we have a much more positive experience this time.

JT: were you a salesman before? (laughs). You make it sound very persuasive. I'd like to believe it but you know how it is ... always get fine words ... we'll see what their actions are when it comes to it.

When JT finished with 'we'll see what their actions are ...' I interpreted that as a signal he had sensed that there was an alternative experience possible to the one he had preunderstanding of. An example of leaders achieving changes in legislation caught his attention and gave an alternative picture of the possible positive outcomes from embracing the methodology. He seemed to be signaling a commitment compliance. His continued concerns about senior leader theories-in-action being different from their espoused theories were still very real and justifiable, but he seemed to be willing to give it a go.

Overcoming Negative Preunderstanding – Creating a Memory of the Future

The first task facing an interventionist is to identify leader preunderstanding and, if it is negative, to decide if they should try and counter this. I have given examples of how I went about this above, but it is not as simple as trying to convince them that the methodology is the opposite of what they think, for example not slow and cumbersome but actually speedy and simple. My research has helped me understand that leaders only retrospectively, and *after* moving from their self-defined ignorance to knowledge, find the methodology fast and simple. We saw examples of this in the leader interviews in Chapter 3 who told of their fast change of thinking but then talked about how it actually took them up to two years. Thus, if leaders I was working with had preunderstanding that the methodology was slow and cumbersome, the solution would not have been to give the false impression that the opposite is the case as this is not what they would experience when first engaging with the methodology. The solution had to be more subtle and involved creating some form of memory of the future which helps leaders sensemake that initially it may feel like it is slow but that they will subsequently come to realize, and believe, that it was actually fast. 'Memory of the future' was a term coined by Ingvar (1985) and refers to the concept that individuals cognitively construct simulations of the future which are stored in their memory. These simulations can be positive or negative and, given the retrospective nature of sensemaking, will influence their present sensemaking of past events that were once their imagined future. In other words I had come to believe that in a postmodern process ontology the first step is to help leaders gain some new postmodern preunderstanding that counters their modernist preunderstanding. Szpunar and Jing (2013) suggest 'anxious individuals do not properly weight neutral or positive alternative outcomes of future events'. If leaders have direct or second-hand negative preunderstanding about the methodology then it is possible that they will feel anxious about it and their thinking about possible outcomes will be skewed by this negative preunderstanding.

There is also a risk of negative reaction to using the second-hand experience of other leaders who have previously engaged with the methodology. Advocates of the methodology may seek to give sense to others that they have a *better* rather than a *different* view of reality. Some advocates who engaged in commitment compliance with the methodology may make sense of the cognitive dissonance it creates for them by interpreting their new thinking and behavior as a better or more accurate reality which they have uncovered by using a different lens, just as the leaders in Chapter 3 did. This interpretation of the better reality then becomes a sensemaking story of insight leading to a better view of reality than that held by their colleagues who have not engaged with the methodology. Their stories may be an attempt to give sense of the methodology to other leaders but which end up being interpreted as arrogance and an attitude of superiority, thus reinforcing the negative preunderstanding of the methodology as telling leaders that they don't know how to lead effectively.

So, seeking to help leader create a memory of the future can be an effective method to help leaders gain new preunderstanding and encourage their continued engagement, but it can also rebound and embed current thinking if not handled carefully.

References

Chia, R. 1994. The concept of decision: A deconstructive analysis. *Journal of Management Studies*, Vol. 31, 781–806.

Chia, R. 1995. From modern to postmodern organizational analysis. *Organization Studies*, Vol. 16, 579–604.

Chia, R. 1996. The problem of reflexivity in organizational research: Towards a postmodern science of organization. *Organization*, Vol. 3, 31–59.

Chia, R. 1997. Essai: Thirty years on: From organizational structures to the organization of thought. *Organization Studies*, Vol. 18, 685–707.

Chia, R. 1999. A 'rhizomic' model of organisational change and transformation: Perspective from a metaphysics of change. *British Journal of Management*, Vol. 10, 209–227.

Chia, R. 2003. Organization theory as a postmodern science. *In:* Tsoukas, H. & Knudsen, C. (eds.) *The Oxford Handbook of Organization Theory: Meta-Theoretical Perspectives*. (pp. 113–142). Oxford: Oxford University Press.

Chia, R. & Holt, R. 2006. Strategy as practical coping: A Heideggarian perspective. *Organization Studies*, Vol. 27, 635–655.

Deming, W. E. 1982. *Out of the Crisis*, Cambridge, MIT CAES.

Deming, W. E. 1994. *The New Economics For Industry, Government, Education*, Cambridge, MIT CAES.

Gummesson, E. 2000. *Qualitative Methods in Management Research*, Thousand Oaks, Sage Publications.

Ingvar, D. H. 1985. Memory of the future: An essay on the temporal organization of conscious awareness. *Human Neurobiology*, Vol. 4, 127–136.

Seddon, J. 2003. *Freedom from Command & Control: A Better Way to Make the Work Work*, Buckingham, Vanguard Education Ltd.

Seddon, J. 2008. *Systems Thinking in the Public Sector: The Failure of the Reform Regime … and a Manifesto for a Better Way*, Axminster, Triarchy Press.

Seddon, J. 2010. Lean is a wicked disease: How service organisations are waking up to the problem. *Vanguard-method Newsletter* [Online]. Available from: www.vanguard-method.net [Accessed 30th June 2012].

Senge, P. M. 1990. *The Fifth Discipline: The Art and Practice of the Learning Organization*, London, Random House.

Senge, P. M. 1992. Mental Models. *Planning Review*, Vol. 20, 4–10.

Senge, P. M., Kleiner, A., Roberts, C., Ross, R., Roth, G. & Smith, B. 1999. *The Dance of Change: The Challenges of Sustaining Momentum in Learning Organizations*, London, Nicholas Brealey Publishing.

Szpunar, K. K. & Jing, H. G. 2013. Memory-mediated simulations of the future: What are the advantages and pitfalls? *Journal of Applied Research in Memory and Cognition*, Vol. 2, 240–242.

8 Cognitive Dissonance

Burning Platform or Has Someone Burnt the Toast?

I have often heard leaders use the phrase 'cognitive dissonance' when they are really talking about difficult decisions, typified by a leader who was telling me about a meeting he had attended and at which 'you could sense the cognitive dissonance as they wrestled with the decision - outsource or not'. This is an example of lax preunderstanding being used by the leader who is aware of the concept of cognitive dissonance but does not properly understand what it is. Choosing an option may be a difficult decision, but that is not the same as cognitive dissonance.

Sensemaking is not about contributing to rational decision-making. It is about retrospectively rationalizing decisions taken, which could even appear to an observer to be quite irrational decisions. So, far from being a logical sequence of steps from interpretation to decision-making to action, the process of sensemaking runs to some degree in reverse. It is more about rationalizing actions already taken. In this sense it shares thinking with cognitive dissonance theory in that it focuses on post-decisional efforts to revise the meaning of decisions that have negative cognitive consequences (Beauvois and Joule, 1996, Festinger, 1957, 1964, Harmon-Jones and Mills, 1999, Harmon-Jones et al., 2003).

Cognitive dissonance is the next element of sensemaking and influences how people generate that which they then make sense of. Cognitive dissonance theory was developed by Festinger (1957) and is both an individual cognitive and a social psychology perspective that has strong relevance to organizational sensemaking. As with sensemaking, it is retrospective, precedes interpretation and concerns rationalizing decisions rather than rational decision making. Festinger's theory of cognitive dissonance proposes that psychological discomfort is created when there is an inconsistency between 'what a person knows or believes and what he does' (Festinger, 1957, p.1). Festinger (1957) replaces the term 'inconsistency' with 'dissonance'. His hypotheses are as follows:

> 1. The existence of dissonance, being psychologically uncomfortable, will motivate the person to try to reduce the dissonance and achieve consonance.
> 2. When dissonance is present, in addition to trying to reduce it, the person will actively avoid situations and information which would likely increase the dissonance.
>
> (p.3)

An example of when dissonance might arise is a smoker who believes smoking is unhealthy, antisocial and professes that s/he wishes to stop, but who keeps on smoking. Espoused beliefs and behaviors conflict and the dissonance can be reduced in three ways:

1. We can change our *behaviors* to align with our beliefs or attitudes, i.e. stop smoking
2. We can change our *beliefs or attitudes* to align with our behaviors, i.e. find lots of arguments of why smoking is acceptable and which outweigh the negative aspect, e.g. smoking helps you relax and lower your blood pressure, it keeps your weight down, and so forth, so actually on balance smoking is good for you.
3. We can add a *new cognitive element* that rationalizes our currently dissonant behaviors and attitudes and renders them consonant e.g. yeah generally speaking smoking is bad for you and I keep smoking *but* my grandfather smoked 20 a day and lived until he was 92 so I probably have his genes which means I can safely smoke cigarettes.

In addition to these three techniques for reducing dissonance there is a link to another sensemaking element – ontology. Festinger (1957) also found that we seek to avoid any increase in dissonance by actively seeking out new information in a highly selective manner and that 'it is well known that people cognize and interpret information to fit what they already believe' (p.150).

Beauvois and Joule (1996) revisited Festinger's theory and found that it had been extensively revised and attempts made to invalidate it by subsequent researchers who had gradually turned it into a theory of the ego and self-perception. They point out that Festinger's original theory:

> ... is not a theory of consistency, since the function of this post-behavioral dissonance reduction process is not to eliminate cognitive inconsistencies (as we shall see, it can even produce them) but to rationalize behavior.
>
> (Beauvois and Joule, 1996, p. xii)

So it is possible for dissonance reduction to leave consistency or inconsistency between other cognitions unchanged and even to create new inconsistencies (such as the belief that just because my grandfather smoked and live to 92 then I can smoke and will live to a good age as well). This is only a problem if Festinger's theory is erroneously taken to be a theory of achieving consistency. It is not, the aim of dissonance reduction is to restore the cognitive 'value' of the behavior, i.e. rationalization of problematic behavior. This rationalizing element of cognitive dissonance reduction is strongly linked to retrospective sensemaking of decisions. Most decisions involve a choice between alternatives which once chosen can lead to cognitive dissonance and its subsequent reduction by enhancing the attractive elements of the chosen alternative and emphasizing the negative features of the rejected alternative. Weick (1995) explains that:

> ... these operations retrospectively alter the meaning of the decision, the nature of the alternatives, and the "history" of the decision in a manner reminiscent of Garfinkel's jurors. In both cases, people start with an outcome in hand – a verdict, a choice – and then render that outcome sensible by constructing a plausible story that produced it (in Garfinkel's words, "the interpretation makes good sense").
>
> (p.11)

Weick is referring to Garfinkel's (1967) study of jurors which found that they decided a remedy (innocence or guilt) and then made sense of this retrospectively by deciding the 'facts' from among different alternative claims that justified the remedy they had chosen. This is an important factor when studying sensemaking of leaders engaging with change interventions. Much of the literature on change focuses on how leaders can overcome resistance (of others) to change but Festinger's and Weick's definitions described earlier suggest that the concept of resistance fades away. There is no resistance, just a decision to go with, or reject, the options for change and each can be made sense of, or rationalized, equally effectively. Alternatively of course it could be argued that the concept of resistance is strengthened because these definitions mean that both sides can legitimately claim the other is the resistor of the correct decision or the appropriate course of action. The point is that trying to pin down who is 'resisting', and what, distracts from the key issue of how decisions are being rationalized by both supporters and detractors of the changes being proposed.

Weick summarizes the legacy of cognitive dissonance theory and its shared ideas with sensemaking by asserting that both:

- involve increasing the number of cognitive elements that are consistent with the decision being made sense of
- entail justification being triggered by the choice made (and so are post-decisional behaviors)

- are retrospective and use post-decision outcomes to reconstruct pre-decisional histories
- are triggered by some form of discrepancy or unexpected outcome
- use social construction of justification
- are founded on the concept that action shapes cognition

I observed these sensemaking actions many times in my work with leaders in the research organizations.

The War Room

I was working with a small group of senior leaders in a large organisation facing an existential crisis following the financial crisis in 2009. They were facing a catastrophic drop in income and were seeking to transform the organization and achieve a multi-million reduction in operating costs. I was employed to work with the small group of leaders (SLT) who had been set up as a project board to evaluate the methodology to get the wider leadership team (WLT) onboard with the transformation approach. On one occasion there was a discussion about how to first engage with the WLT:

BB: I think what'll happen is we'll meet short, quickly, often, whoever needs to, and on a regular basis we'll be all in one place to go and get where are we, what we think's happening, does anybody agree with what this looks like, I can't get any response from such and such, can you fix it for me. All of that kind of stuff is going to be banging off, and like a war room really.

BB: Have you read Kotter's 'Our Iceberg is Melting'?

RJ: Brilliant, brilliant little book ... the whole thing is penguins, a penguin realizes that the iceberg they're on is melting but nobody believes him cos it's a big secure environment, you know, this penguin gets ostracized and .... So it's a fable about change. So I just thought some of the comments are kind of quite systemic and quite typical of people who are fearful of change. And the mantra of this is philosophy (laughs) ... it's about learning and improvement and ... so the summary is, but actually are we convinced that our iceberg is melting? Is there a burning platform?[1]

DD: yeah ... most [of the WLT] haven't really got the seriousness of what's happening or how short the timescale is. They're so focused on surviving this year's budget cuts they are kind of 'let's worry about next year's nearer the time'.

Me: that's the trouble with melting ... it creeps up on you then holy shit the iceberg's now just an ice cube!

BB: yeah so we need to act fast to show them the iceberg's melting ... or umm ... the platform's burning .... Whichever version you like (laughs).

This exchange illustrates a number of important aspects in the SLT's sensemaking of how to engage the WLT in the methodology

- Preunderstanding (which I covered in Chapter 7)
- Use of metaphors as a storytelling tool
- An attempt to create cognitive dissonance

BB refers to Kotter and Rathgeber's (2005) iceberg change fable book and then brings in one of the steps from Kotter's (1996) change model – the need to create a sense of urgency, which BB calls a burning platform, i.e. a sense that the situation is so critical that clear and urgent change is required. Notwithstanding the mixed metaphors of melting icebergs and burning platforms, they were used by the group for establishing a collective sense of the need for quick action along the lines of Kotter's change model.

This use of metaphors as a storytelling and sensemaking trope is something that was evident throughout my research. They provide a useful shortcut to help establish shared understanding and BB's use of the melting iceberg and burning platform mixed metaphors were examples of this social sensemaking, but these sort of shortcuts via the use of metaphors are based on an assumption that everyone has the same understanding of the metaphor (since if it had to be explained in detail there would be no shortcut). In this case no one questioned the metaphor and it seemed to me that there was implicit understanding of Kotter and his change method simply from the use of iceberg and burning platform references and shared understanding of what these meant.

BB had mentioned setting up a war room. This militaristic metaphor was also accepted by the group without discussion about what he meant by it. A room was allocated for the group to use as the war room - a base to meet and collate the evidence that wider leadership group would be confronted with in order to generate cognitive dissonance when they realized that their espoused leadership theories and their theories in action were fundamentally mismatched. We hoped that this would create an opportunity for them to accept that their current thinking was flawed and needed to change:

AA: We use the war room to present, to give a picture, that says actually say the fact that, you know, we've found our savings, but you're going to have to change your thinking - a *lot*. At the moment ... they're, they're buffered and shielded from the harsh reality of what's actually happening on the ground. This process

> ... if we get it right, will actually put a ring through their nose and drag 'em right into 'this is what's actually going on in [the organization'.

The group recognized the importance of getting the Chief Executive on board and leading the methodology if the rest of the leaders were going to be influenced enough to also engage:

AA: Where I think we can pull him in though is through the war room. If he gets it he can push the Program Board, because I think if he gets the Program Board lined up to challenge as well as have expectations about making decisions and making sure that the decisions are implemented, you know, I think it will expose the, you know, the non-compliers, if you want to put it in that way, or the strugglers who may need to step outside comfort zones and do something else to really sort of get to grips.

At this stage there was still some sensemaking taking place around the issue of leader support or resistance to engaging with the methodology and AA was resurfacing these concerns. At first the phrase was non-compliers which implies some form of conscious resistance. But then AA said 'or the strugglers' which to me is different from non-compliance. The methodology challenges leaders to change long-held mindsets and it should not be surprising that some will struggle with that. BB appeared to sense this difference as well:

BB: the thing I've learned ... is some of the individuals that I would think of as a bit Machiavellian, ... I actually think it's their antidote to the organization ... cos they know they can't possibly do anything in this organization to make anything happen, so if we give them a real chance we might see different behavior from them.

We concluded that we were not facing active resistance and instead sensed the opportunity to create some heretical thinking. A comprehensive data gathering exercise was undertaken the war room walls covered in charts, slides, data tables, picture and other visuals. We agreed that it presented a comprehensive picture of the problems that current leadership thinking was causing and the need for radical change. We were focused on demonstrating the key heresy of leadership – that organizational performance is a direct result of leader mindsets about leading and organizing. One example of this 'leader thinking determines the system which determines performance' cycle that was displayed in the war room related to the spans and tiers of control in the organization. A chart which we felt would be particularly shocking for WLT members was an analysis of the hierarchy and tiers of management in the organization which showed a top-heavy management and support structure with only 38% of employees in customer facing roles and 62% in supervisory, management, leadership and support roles.

Over a period of a week WLT members were given individual tours of the war room and the outcome was universal hostility and rejection. I list here a few of the representative comments made by leaders and which I interpret as most relevant to their sensemaking:

- GM – you're just cherry-picking data and sticking it on the wall - it only paints half the picture. I could show you lots of stuff that says we are doing very well ... I can see some interesting stuff but there's no coherent story.
- GL – I don't accept how you define failure demand. They [customers] might be phoning in about other things but you've recorded here as failure demand (referring to 66% failure demand from customers).
- TD – intuitively you will get more complaints about those services anyway because it's more visible.
- SD – isn't it just a matter of extent? You'd expect complaints about [services].
- DB – No, no, no. You're just emphasizing 'crazy' examples of ownership of [services] or who does what – overall it's sensible across [the organization].
- SH – we've known about these things for a while. To be honest you're not telling us anything we didn't know.
- SH – a lot of the data is just interpretation and not the real picture
- GL – let's face it, no system will ever be 100% perfect.
- GL – the figures are wrong - you can't have quality and lower costs. You're wanting a Rolls Royce for the price of a Skoda.
- ST – the big savings are in [another department's] budget – just cut that and leave the rest alone if you want to make savings.
- MB – charge customers to inspect the stuff they complain about – most your figures [failure demand] are just time wasters.
- WS – we've wasted six weeks to get this? This doesn't tell us anything. Most the information isn't relevant and the rest is just plain wrong.
- GB – all this stuff about our thinking causing these problems, it's not right. You're trying to pin blame on us for the world we live in. It's easy to fantasize about how much better things would be but you don't have to deliver the hard reality. Making us the whipping boy might make them [staff] feel better but it isn't going to solve the problems. If this is what systems [the methodology] is about we've just wasted six weeks.
- HE – I take exception to this [war room data]. It's a disgrace. You're just trying to make us look bad and your data is skewed. [I

asked in what way and she pointed to the hierarchy slide] You're just trying to stir up trouble. I sometimes have to speak to a customer if they escalate a complaint so I'm frontline but you're trying to make out that I don't do anything for customers. I'm really angry.

- LD – that [frontline/mgt hierarchy] slide has to go. All organizations have a lot of support staff and you're making us look worse than it is. It can't stay.

We had hoped the war room data would create the burning platform and that the overwhelming evidence would prevent leaders rationalizing it away, but rationalizing is exactly what they did. Instead of shocking CLT members into engaging more with the methodology it seemed to have antagonized them, turned them against it and reinforced their current thinking.

Examining the reactions there appear to be two contradictory sensemaking themes:

1. It's true but we already knew this. Rationalize the data with 'so what' sweeping statements such as every organization has a lot of support staff, thereby undermining the idea that this is in some way a problem that they should be thinking about differently.
2. It's not true and we don't accept it. Find fault with the data in order to undermine it or claim that it is in some way fake, biased or skewed and so has no credibility.

Some of the CLT members seemed able to harmonize these apparently contradictory themes within their own sensemaking:

- HE says that the data is only half the picture, suggesting that the problem is not the accuracy of the data, just that there is not enough of it. But HE also says that the data is wrong.
- GL says that 'no system is perfect' which suggests that he is not arguing with the data, just whether there is a problem with it. However, like HE he also then questions the data.
- SH says he's not learned anything new and that he's known about the data for a long time, but also then says the data is wrong.

These examples seem to evidence that, in the circumstances of the war room, sensemaking was rationalizing rather than rational behavior. Thus, there is no problem on the one hand saying it's true and they knew this all along but on the other hand it's not true and so essentially worthless. It may not seem rational, but it rationalizes their current thinking and their rejection of the need to change their thinking, i.e. it resolves any cognitive dissonance discomfort.

I also spoke to GL who had expressed the opinions that he already knew what he was seeing but also that the data were wrong:

Me: I'd like to better understand your thoughts on the war room visit because I know you weren't very happy with the data.

GL: yeah, I told you that you hadn't produced anything we didn't already know.

Me: but some of the data hasn't been produced before and we had to manually extract it so I'm not sure how [he knew].

GL: I don't need fine detail to know what's happening. Everyone knows the issues.

Me: I see, but I recall you suggesting that some of the data that we collected was wrong?

GL: Yeah, all that stuff about failure demand, it's just a question of how you view it. People complain all the time and you're not going to stop that. I've got one bloke in [name of area] who's mission in life is to be a pain in the neck. He spends all his time complaining and I have to waste time drafting replies basically telling him [complaint handler] that the guy's an idiot. The world's coming to an end and your spending six weeks telling me I've got idiots like him. Tell me something I don't know.

Me: DB said we were emphasizing crazy examples but haven't you just done the same. Our data was collected over six weeks and thousands of customer interactions and relates to frequent 'normal' complaints we are getting.

GL: I don't need any of that to know what the problem is. We've got to cut the budget and I'll do that. How the rest do it is up to them but I'll present the savings that are needed and I don't need [the methodology] to do that.

GL's responses were similar to other leaders. The questioning of the data was not because he felt it was wrong per se but rather defensive reasoning of the surfacing of the unsayable (defensive reasoning is another sensemaking element and I cover this in Chapter 10). If he already knew the data why was he apparently hostile to it? It seems that being known is not the same as in the open. When I spoke about the volume of data GL said he didn't need the 'fine detail' and the problem was that we were surfacing things that didn't need surfaced because he already had solutions for them. In my own sensemaking of the conversation I felt that, unlike HE, the data were not seen particularly as a threat to GL (he was confident he had solutions that would solve his problems and he wasn't interested in how the others would solve theirs), but it did present a potential loss of face. The data about poor customer experience of his services led to defensive reasoning centered around avoiding this loss of face.

The war room was discussed at a meeting of the full leadership group and feedback on this came from AA:

AA: they were rubbishing the transformation agenda saying things like 'it won't work', 'it won't deliver', 'there isn't the time to do it' etc. etc. I think some of them got it and wanted to use the war room data to open a discussion about doing things differently but there was no support from the Chief Exec and some of them pre-empted any discussion by announcing their own 'transformation' projects that would make the necessary savings. They're just more salami slicing of course but CE didn't take them on so there was no room for anyone else to challenge them when they were promising the savings. Of course they couldn't dismiss it out of hand so it was left at let's get some more detail on what the solutions would look like.

BB: I spent 2 hours driving home after it and all of it was spent reflecting on what had happened. They all as usual had talked far too much about irrelevant stuff that avoided talking about the data. Also, it's clear we don't have many supporters.

AA: They were saying that, you know, this is nothing, you have seen it all before, you know, or I'd like to say…

BB: It's fascinating though, if they're seeing it, you know, don't appear to be doing anything about it.

AA: That's what I wanted to say (laughter) and I didn't say it. You know, if you've seen it all before why haven't you changed it?

Me: I've been asked to prepare a discussion document about [one of the war room suggestions for redesign] as 'they were interested in knowing more about our thinking on this'.

All: (lots of laughter) … that's code for we don't like it and kick it into the long grass.

DD: (laughs) yeah that's their way of saying they want nothing to do with it! Write us a report and it will never be heard of again.

CC: It defies belief, despite overwhelming evidence that what we're currently doing isn't working, we're going to persist in doing it, just less of it!'

DD: they are increasingly adopting a 'moving the deck chairs on the Titanic' approach. Not only are they moving them about – they're actually adding more!

BB: the Titanic hasn't got a captain – he went down before the ship. We saw the iceberg coming two years ago but we still haven't managed to change course because we're still arguing about whether to turn to port or starboard!'

AA: most still don't realize how serious the situation is and are focused on protecting their own areas. We're suffering from [the Chief Executive] not giving them a sense of urgency or burning platform or making some grand gestures like sacking one or two senior people who are resisting.

BB: another burning platform?? I expected to hear people talking about this burning platform [at the war room] but all I can hear is 'sniff ... sniff ... has someone burnt the toast?

The meeting had provided an opportunity for some social sensemaking. There was general consensus that the war room exercise had been a disaster and far from creating a burning platform, had reinforced current thinking. From a sensemaking perspective I was curious about *why* leaders would rationalize seemingly irrational beliefs and behaviors. The answer lies in cognitive dissonance theory and understanding what I call the Goldilocks principle. We had sought to create cognitive dissonance in the war room but had failed to understand that cognitive dissonance only occurs when behaviors and attitudes are dissonant and since we had failed to engage the leaders in collecting the data and making it 'their' data they were able to rationalize what they had seen and there was no cognitive dissonance.

The Goldilocks Principle of Cognitive Dissonance

Thus, I had learned that using a modernist change methodology to gain leader commitment to a postmodern methodology was unlikely to result in leader engagement. I suggest that there is a Goldilocks principle of cognitive dissonance linked to their degree of commitment compliance (which I cover in Chapter 9). If there is no leader engagement because leaders delegate the change initiative to others to deal with, there is no cognitive dissonance because there is no behavior on their part to cause inconsistency. The consequence is that leaders are unlikely to perceive a need for change in mindset. Even limited behavioral engagement in the form of leaders controlling the initiative through a project board also results in too little cognitive dissonance when they are confronted with data that they have not been involved in collecting and which is inconsistent with their espoused leadership behaviors. We saw this when we thought that creating a sense of urgency or burning platform (Kanter, 1983, 1989, Kotter, 1996, Kotter and Rathgeber, 2005) and confronting leaders with counter-attitudinal data as we did in the war room would create cognitive dissonance and lead leaders to reject the methodology and reinforce their current mindsets as predicted by cognitive dissonance theory (Beauvois and Joule, 1996, Festinger, 1957). The 'just the right amount' balance requires leader commitment compliance to engage in actively collecting counter-attitudinal data that expose an inconsistency between their espoused behaviors and their behaviors in action. They must have agreed to engage in collecting the data for the cognitive dissonance to arise – someone else collecting it and presenting it to them will not suffice.

In subsequent research organizations I sought to avoid a repeat of what had happened in the war room example and instead generate a 'just right' level of cognitive dissonance that created an opportunity for leaders to reflect on and change their mindsets. Notwithstanding that I believed I had an understanding of the need to avoid too little or too much dissonance, identifying the 'just right' amount in an organizational setting whilst working with many individuals and with many confounding variables is not a straightforward task. The methodologies I was using seek to address this issue by emphasizing that senior leaders must engage with the initial data gathering and cannot delegate this to others, but I and the rest of our small group had ignored this principle in the war room example and allowed the leaders to delegate it to us to project manage. In subsequent interventions I ensured that I took leaders through a structured action learning and reflexive practice cycle which sought to engage leaders in creating their own dissonance inducing data by incrementally building a picture that they could not rationalize from within their current mindset. Essentially the methodologies reverse modernist thinking in which a melting iceberg approach is the problem and a burning platform the solution. My postmodern-based approach was designed to create a melting iceberg of data gathering which the leaders themselves then use retrospectively to create a burning platform, not by having others (as we tried in the war room example) strike a match and set the platform ablaze beneath them.

Note

1 Kotter's (1996) 8 step change model has 'create a sense of urgency' as step 2 and Kotter talks about the need to use crises to create a burning platform that forces people to jump off their current comfort zone platform. In my experience, leaders familiar with Kotter's model usually use the term burning platform rather than the term create a sense of urgency.

References

Beauvois, J.-L. & Joule, R.-V. 1996. *A Radical Dissonance Theory*, London, Taylor and Francis.

Festinger, L. 1957. *A Theory of Cognitive Dissonance*, Stanford, Stanford University Press.

Festinger, L. 1964. Behavioral support for opinion change. *The Public Opinion Quarterly*, Vol. 28, 404–417.

Garfinkel, H. 1967. *Studies in Ethnomethodology*, Englewood Cliffs, Prentice Hall.

Harmon-Jones, E. & Mills, J. (eds.) 1999. *Cognitive Dissonance: Progess on a Pivotal Theory in Social Psychology*, Washington: American Psychological Association.

Harmon-Jones, E., Peterson, H. & Vaughn, K. 2003. The dissonance-inducing effects of an inconsistency between experienced empathy and knowledge of past failures to help: Support for the action-based model of dissonance. *Basic and Applied Social Psychology*, Vol. 25, 69–78.

Kanter, R. M. 1983. *The Change Masters: Innovation & Entrepreneurship in the American Corporation*, New York, Simon & Schuster Inc.

Kanter, R. M. 1989. *When Giants Learn to Dance: Mastering the Challenges of Strategy, Management, and Careers in the 1990s*, London, Unwin.

Kotter, J. P. 1996. *Leading Change*, Boston, Harvard Business School Press.

Kotter, J. P. & Rathgeber, H. 2005. *Our Iceberg is Melting: Changing and Succeeding Under Any Conditions*, London, MacMillan.

Weick, K. E. 1995. *Sensemaking in Organizations*, London, Sage Publications.

9 Commitment Compliance – A Fusion of Forced Free Will

The next sensemaking element is closely linked to cognitive dissonance. It forms the bridge between, on the one hand, our current ontology and preunderstanding and, on the other, our ownership of change in mindset and, to use the metaphors of the leaders we have heard from, our irreversible crossing of the Rubicon to a new reality. This 'bridge' consists of leader agreement to engage with the methodology, even although at this stage they know very little about it or may even hold negative preunderstanding. But as an interventionist what do I mean by agreement to engage – complying or committing? Actually I mean elements of both.

Commitment is defined as a pledge or undertaking, an obligation that restricts freedom of action, whereas compliance is defined as the act of complying with a wish or command, excessive acquiescence. The term 'forced compliance' is frequently used by theorists of cognitive dissonance (Aronson, 1992, 1997, Bacharach et al., 1996, Festinger, 1957, Harmon-Jones and Mills, 1999) and commitment v compliance was a concept used by many of the leaders I worked with during my research. Many of the leaders talked to me about how important it is in their role as sense*givers* to get staff commitment to change rather than forced compliance because forced compliance gets adoption of the desired behaviors only as long as leader attention is being paid to the behavior. As soon as leaders move their attention to something else staff will revert to old behaviors because they are not committed to the new behaviors, i.e. their mindset has not changed. However, the leaders use of the terms in a way which suggests commitment is freely given and compliance is a forced action does not accurately reflect cognitive dissonance theory since commitment can restrict freedom to act and compliance can be freely given. To avoid confusion in my work with organizational leaders I used a fusion of the concepts of commitment and compliance by using the term commitment compliance. There was a pragmatic reason for this – leaders tended to react negatively to any discussion about their forced compliance in engaging with the methodology as it seemed to create a feeling of some sort of loss of face by challenging their authority. They were senior leaders in their organizations and how dare I suggest they could be 'forced' into engaging with the methodology.

Creating the Goldilocks 'just right' amount of cognitive dissonance that I discussed in Chapter 8 requires leaders to sense that they have freedom of choice on whether to engage with the methodology or not but this freedom cannot be all that it seems and entails their compliance:

> We shall not speak of freedom or even the feeling of freedom but of the statement of freedom. The experimenter states (or does not state) that the subject is free to take part or not take part in the experimental situation. We can describe this situation as a situation of compliance since it implies the subject's obedience to an agent (the experimenter) who makes a problematic demand and who possesses a certain degree of authority. Once this situation has been accepted, the behaviour of the subject is and remains at the discretion of the experimenter
>
> (Beauvois and Joule, 1996, p.49)

Beauvois and Joule are describing laboratory experiments on cognitive dissonance, but their statement is equally relevant in the setting of organizations. In the laboratory the experimenter in symbolic white coat is the figure of authority, whereas in organizations the figure of authority is the interventionist whose 'white coat' is expertise and credibility in the eyes of the leaders. The problematic demand made of leaders is that they commit to engaging with a methodology they know little about but which they have been told will challenge their current thinking about organizing and leading:

> Commitment to an act is a necessary condition (but insufficient, because the act must also be discomforting, i.e. counterattitudinal or countermotivational) for induction of a state of dissonance.
>
> (Beauvois and Joule, 1999, p.63)

I demonstrated the outcome of failing to gain leader commitment compliance in Chapter 8 where we tried to compensate for the lack of commitment compliance by using the war room to generate cognitive dissonance instead. Not only did it fail to generate cognitive dissonance, but it also reinforced current leader thinking. In subsequent interventions I was careful to address this sensemaking element early on. As an interventionist I cannot create, measure and manipulate cognitive dissonance ratios and formulae as can be done in a laboratory under strictly controlled experimental conditions. Nevertheless, as part of imparting new preunderstanding to leaders regarding the methodology I am careful to establish my credibility as expert in using the methodology in similar leadership roles to themselves.

Having created my virtual 'lab white coat' with leaders in subsequent interventions in the research I then proceeded to negotiate pragmatic engagement which included the same elements that all leaders are asked to commit to:

- Attending the majority of daily team learning reviews,
- actively taking part in each of the key stages of data gathering such as listening to customer demand, mapping flows etc.
- leading the identification of systems conditions and leader thinking causing them
- leading the identification of changes in thinking required and presenting to wider leadership team
- leading experiments in new forms of organizing and leading

Each of these activities is part of a data gathering jigsaw puzzle that builds a complete picture of their current mindset and the impact that it is having. I stressed to leaders at the outset that it is not a 'pick and mix' approach in which leaders can choose which bits to engage in, and achieving their understanding and agreement to this constitutes the commitment compliance that is a precursor of creating cognitive dissonance.

Over the period of my research I found that there were two common issues that had a strong impact on leader initial commitment compliance and on their subsequent delivery on that commitment.

What Does 'Full Time' Mean?

A common stumbling block to gaining commitment compliance from leaders was the issue of what they understood 'engagement' to mean. Senior leaders are extremely busy people and telling them they would have to clear their diaries in order to actively lead the intervention seemed to make no sense when they had 'business as usual' to run alongside the deconstruction of their current concepts of leadership and organization during the initial phases of the methodology. So I had to develop a pragmatic approach based on gaining leader commitment compliance to an 'appropriate' level of presence in the intervention team that allowed a balancing act between leading the old world and simultaneously deconstructing it in order to construct a new world of organizing and leading. However, I also learned that interpreting, and trying to influence, leader sensemaking is far from straightforward, as when I learned the importance of language and the impact just one word can have.

I worked with one group of leaders in an organization where we very nearly reached the same impasse as I had with the leaders in the war room example because of just one word. I had established their pre-understanding, which was word of mouth from colleagues and had been largely negative. I had presented them positive preunderstanding examples from my own experience and they had accepted these alternatives as realistic options so I felt we were close to agreeing their commitment compliance to engage in a period of reflexive action learning. I used a PowerPoint slide to list the logistical issues we would need to address if we were to proceed and as the meeting progressed, I noticed that the most senior leader was not looking happy. He was letting the other leaders do the talking, and his body language made me feel that he was not supportive – crossed arms, frowns, some shaking of the head. Nevertheless, things seemed to be going well and so I decided not to test my assumptions in case I was misinterpreting his thinking. There was positive discussion about the staff we would need to release from their current roles in order to engage in a full-time data gathering exercise that could last up to six weeks. It was when I initiated a discussion about the leader's role in the data gathering that the language problem surfaced. I had used the term 'full-time' for the team in the data gathering exercise but had deliberately use the word 'necessary' to describe the expectation of the senior leader's time commitment to the intervention. When it came to discussing the senior leader role it became clear I had good reason to think he looked unhappy:

PS: I think there's a problem here. It's going to cause a lot of problems for me but I'm prepared to pull them [the staff allocated to the intervention] out of the work but I think you're unrealistic about asking me to do the same. I have to keep this business running and I'm happy to support the intervention but you can't possibly expect me to just clear my diary for six weeks. I've got important meetings with strategic stakeholders coming up, I've got presentations to give that the Chief Exec has asked me to give ... are you expecting me to say 'sorry not doing now coz I'm cancelling everything for six weeks'? It's not realistic and if your saying it's that or no intervention then so be it.

I was taken aback by this because it was clear that PS's sensemaking of what he'd been listening to was that he was being asked to devote himself full-time to the intervention despite my attempt to separate his and the rest of the team's level of time commitment. I had talked about full-time for the team and the necessary time for him to lead and support the team but what he had heard was me asking him to sign up to full-time engagement for six weeks. So despite my attempt to avoid the trap of being seen to be unrealistic about senior leader time commitment, the word 'necessary' was sensed by PS as a synonym for full time since this is what we had been discussing for everyone else. We were at a point where the senior leader was ready to walk away from the intervention because of my failure to give him a sense of a more pragmatic engagement in terms of his time.

I wondered why PS had waited until this point to raise his concerns since he had allowed the meeting to discuss and agree full-time commitment of other leaders and staff, but I didn't feel asking this at that point would help me recover the situation. I sought to defuse the situation by saying that I hadn't been as clear as I should have been and that I fully understood that he had to manage the business while simultaneously supporting the intervention. I then explained that this was why I had used the word 'necessary' and explained that what was important was that PS was 100% committed to leading the intervention but that in terms of his time this might only mean 50% and then discussed the key dates and times that he would be expected to clear his diary to be in the intervention. I asked about the key meetings he had talked about and discussed how these could be accommodated while still allowing him to lead the intervention. This recovery discussion took an hour but by the end PS seemed to have thought through what he was being asked to do and moved from a statement of non-compliance to commitment compliance:

PS: ok well yes of course I think as long as there's a recognition that I have a job to do keeping this business running and not seeing a nose-dive in performance because I walk away for six weeks then of course I want to do the right thing in leading the intervention. It seemed to me you were asking me to clear my diary for six weeks but if we can work around my other commitments then I'm of course happy to do what needs to be done. I can ask about maybe moving some of these stakeholder meetings around.

PS seemed to have been reassured enough to commit to engaging with, and leading, the intervention. He had moved from the challenge of 'so be it' to the much more positive 'I want to do the right thing'. His sensemaking of what was being asked of him may have led him to move from believing that the stakeholder meetings were immoveable to actually perhaps they could be moved. An alternative interpretation could be that he always believed this but made them immoveable as part of his non-compliance position. If so, his sensemaking nevertheless left him confident enough to surface the option that had previously remained unsaid. PS then said something which seemed almost a throwaway remark to him but had an impact on my own ongoing sensemaking:

PS: And of course the other thing is it's not just me ... these guys [other leaders] are being asked to work full-time but there's full-time and there's full-time. I think you mean full-time as 9 to 5 but that's not full-time. Full-time for us is much longer than that and is often eight in the morning to 8 at night. So the reality is we'll be doing stuff before and after the intervention each day and I'll be the same.

PS was pointing out that senior leaders in the organization regularly work long hours and so would be able to do some 'old world' work before and after the time they spent in the intervention team. For me however, this relatively simple observation was a significant moment in my own continuous stream of sensemaking. This was the second time that the phrase full-time had caused me difficulties and now I could see that part of the problem was my binary perception of full-time or part-time. Saying the team would be full time and the leader not, was creating a false separation. PS's observation helped me reflect on this thinking. Time is a continuous stream and the concept of full-time is whatever the user of the term chooses to bracket in this continuous stream. PS was quite right in that my full-time was 9am-5pm each day, whereas his full-time was more like 8am-8pm each day. The learning for me was that use of the phrase full-time could give the wrong sense to senior leaders and I should avoid it altogether. In future I talked about appropriate time commitment of everyone involved and then discussed what this might look like.

But We're Different

Time commitment was one issue that required me to give leaders a sense of pragmatic engagement with the methodology if I was to get their commitment compliance, but it was not the only issue. HL was representative of other leaders whose thinking, often because of preunderstanding about the methodology, was discouraging them from moving to commitment compliance. After talking about a visit to see the methodology in action in another organization I was encouraged by his positive views on what he had seen. However, after saying how impressed he was he went on to say

> 'I could see how it has transformed their operations so when I was asked if we'd do it I was like 'ok who wouldn't want to do what they did' ... but we're a different type of business and I think we've got different customers and business models and processes so I'm not sure it would work for us.

HL was sensemaking that the methodology was about process and organizational design. He was impressed by what had happened in the call center he had visited, but his business was not a call center so the same organizational design and processes would not work in his business. The effort put into giving him positive preunderstanding had failed to address a key sensemaking issue, which is that the methodology is about leader mindset not about process or organizational design. HL was correct in his thinking that his caseload-driven insurance claims business was different from the transactional sales contact center he had visited, he was also correct in thinking that the process and organizational redesign that the methodology had led to in the contact center would not be appropriate for his business. What had not been made clear to him was that the methodology was about challenging his current mindset. Any subsequent changes in organizational design and process would flow from this change in mindset and at the outset of engaging with the methodology it would not be possible to say what changes this would lead to in his own business area. This expectation of knowing outcomes from the outset of an initiative is indicative of modernist thinking about change as an epi-phenomenon project with predetermined outcomes.

HL was not the only leader with this 'but we're different' rationalizing resulting from sensemaking that the methodology might be wonderful in other areas of the business but wouldn't work in theirs. My own experience before and during the research was that this was a significant and common problem when trying to gain leader commitment compliance. The rationalizing was largely the same in each case: I'm sure it works in other areas, but we are different or special in some way.

My initial sense was that trying to get the leaders to sense that the methodology was about mindset change not process improvement when they had not yet engaged, or even committed to engage, with the methodology would create confusion. However, I also felt that focusing on practical application of the methodology was exactly the reason that leader's sense of it was of process improvement. So I first sought to give them preunderstanding of application of the methodology in diverse types of business areas using my own experience and which I thought would enhance my credibility as an expert with whom they could commit to work. Secondly, after establishing the methodology had practical application in any business area, I then sought to give leaders a sense of the importance of their own thinking and mindset in determining the outcomes of engaging with the methodology.

In each case I explained that I had worked with leaders using the methodology in three broad categories of business:

1. High volume transactional environments such as contact centers.
2. Long-tail caseload environments such as motor, health or legal claims.
3. Complex one-off project environments such as capital works projects.

I talked through examples of each of these types of business and the results that they had achieved. I explained that the underlying methodology remained the same but the leader findings, redesign of the organization and change in leadership were all different. I emphasized that my role was to coach them in guided action learning and that the outcomes of engaging with this were entirely owned by the leaders and stemmed from thinking differently about how to structure and lead their business. I spent considerable time discussing and explaining this last aspect as it seemed to me that this was the stumbling block that needed to be overcome to prevent leaders feeling they were being shoe-horned into an existing and inappropriate solution.

My learning from these experiences was that, whether because of their own preunderstanding or the preunderstanding opportunities set up as part of my initial interaction with leaders, a significant proportion of leaders will sensemake that they and their business areas are different or special and that therefore the methodology is not appropriate for them. I discussed my experiences of this with TD, a leader I had worked previously and his sense of it was that:

TD: the thing is Ron, every time you try to work with a bunch of leaders you're essentially up against a bunch of NIMBYs[1]. They'll happily tell you how beneficial [the methodology] would be in just about everybody else's area but not theirs. 'We're different, won't work here, not my back yard ... why don't you go over there and do it instead'. And before you say anything, yes I know I was one of them (laughs) ... poacher turned gamekeeper I am so I know what they'll be like (laughs).

What TD said did reflect my own experience on many occasions and after a period reflecting both for this research and my own practitioner development I changed my approach to initial engagement to ensure that any site visit was to a complementary business area and I sought to preempt leader sensemaking about their business being different by surfacing and discussing the three types of business areas in which the methodology has been used. Once I felt leaders had accepted my credibility and the potential relevance of the methodology to their business area I then focused on helping them understand that the methodology was about challenging their current leadership mindset and that they would own the resulting changes in organizing and leading rather than it being about me trying to apply some predetermined 'off the shelf' organizational or process redesign.

Initial Commitment Compliance Does Not Guarantee Continued Compliance

Gaining leaders' commitment compliance does not guarantee that they will actually follow through on their commitments. JS typified the problems in getting leaders to stick to the commitments they have previously given. The first indication of a problem was when he failed to attend the daily team learning reviews. I spoke to him and asked why he had not attended the sessions:

JS: I was asked to attend meetings by [CEO] and couldn't say no. I think the team are capable of doing it without me and I'll catch up when I get into the team. I'm fully committed to this Ron but sometimes strategic priorities get in the way. I'll be in the team this week though.

Me: I see, [CEO] knows you are leading this intervention but have you told him about the need to be available for the learning reviews and if so did you push back when he asked you to attend his meeting? Maybe he didn't realize it clashed with the time you've committed to be in the team?

JS: It's not that simple Ron, my diary is pulled and pushed every hour. I can't tell you what will happen this afternoon never mind next week. I absolutely will clear time to attend the team but I just can't promise that on a given day that won't have to change. I am in contact with [member of the team] regularly and he's keeping me up to date on what's happening

Me: Well there's two issues there really, first is the signal you are sending about the priority of this intervention and your commitment to it if you don't turn up or cancel at short notice. Secondly is that the methodology is about leadership thinking and if you're not in the room you're not there to challenge your thinking.

JS: Ok I get that and I'll be in the team this week

JS didn't turn up to the team that week and only made two short 'drop in' visits in the six weeks of data gathering. My own sense was that JS did want to be supportive and had been genuine when he committed to engaging with the methodology. But as a director and board member of the organization his current reality was that he was under a great deal of time pressure. The issue for me was that his sense of what he had committed to may have been genuine and aligned with what I understood him to be agreeing to, but when put under pressure in his existing world, time to deconstruct and reconstruct his business was deprioritized and ended up being sacrificed. In a laboratory experiment when a participant agrees to commit to the experiment their engagement (unless they choose to withdraw at some point) is guaranteed and there are unlikely to be external interruptions from friends, family or colleagues asking them to do something else. In organizations the pressures on senior leader time are immense and this is a factor that will impact their commitment compliance.

The outcome of non-engagement was predictable. In each case when presented with the findings of the data gathering exercise the sensemaking outcomes were similar to those of the senior leaders in the war room example. The findings came as something of a shock to the leaders and they retreated into rationalizing and defensive behaviors, two while damning the work of the team with faint praise and one with hostility. JS was an example of the faint praise response as this abridged note of his summing up at the end of the presentation demonstrates:

JS: you guys have done a fantastic job and you are a credit to the company. I want to thank you for all the work you've done and the effort you've put in ... you've given us some great insight into our systems and how you can improve them ... I want you to lead on improving our processes and giving our customers a great service. You can rest assured that I will give you whatever support you need to do that.

This apparently supportive summary contains indications that JS's sensemaking has not led to any significant change of mindset. He starts with 'you guys' which is an acknowledgement that it was not 'we' because he failed to engage with the methodology as agreed, however valid his sensemade reasons. He then says the team have given him great insight into how 'you' can improve his systems. This is evidence that JS has not understood the key aspect of the methodology, i.e. that leader thinking determines the system and that improvements to the system require changes in senior leader thinking. Instead, JS is using his pre-understanding of change as a project and delegating process improvement to the team. At the presentation the team had surfaced the key leadership heresies (leader thinking that needed changed) but JS made no reference to these. The team were left feeling they had said the unsayable and JS's ignoring of them meant that he wanted them to remain unsayable.

In another organization a senior leader (JT) had given commitment compliance but then found reasons why she could not follow through on her commitments. She professed to be keeping up to date with progress but when presented with the results of the data gathering appeared shocked and reacted aggressively. As the team started to share their findings they were cut off by JT:

JT: I think we know most of this can you just jump straight to your recommendations please.

The team were taken aback that JT was dismissive of the data they had uncovered as something she already knew, but even although she had not listened to any of the data they moved on to identifying the thinking that needed to change. JT's reaction was:

JT: The trouble is you keep singing the same old song, isn't it about time you found a new tune? You keep telling me there are problems but you don't solve them. There's no point keeping asking me to

> sort out your problems but if that's what you want, I'll do that although you better not complain when I do it.

JT's response contained a number of sensemaking indicators. She had said at the start of the presentation that she knew most of this (although she hadn't heard what the team had uncovered) and now she was re-inforcing her belief that she was hearing nothing new by complaining that her leaders were singing the same old song. She hadn't heard the evidence the team had uncovered and the changes in mindset, which they were suggesting were needed, were not something that had been surfaced with her before. Nevertheless, JT was rationalizing that it had been. I spoke to the two leaders who had presented the data and asked them what they thought the 'same old song' was a reference to:

HS: well if she'd actually been in the team to learn this stuff herself she'd know there was a lot of insight to help her. But I think she thought that because we've raised problems with her in the past and said she needs to change how she thinks about the business that we were just repeating that stuff. But that was about things like staffing levels and IT investment, not fundamentally questioning how we lead the business.

SC: hmmm ... I'm not so sure. I think she did know where we were going with this and by jumping straight to the recommendations she could dismiss it as same old song. But anyway, even if it is the same old song, if she doesn't like it, she's the one who pays the piper so it's up to her to change the tune. She's obviously got no intention of changing anything.

JT's 'you' keep singing the same old song is similar to JS's 'you' can solve the problems. It suggests that she has not grasped that her thinking and her mindset change are the key issues. Instead, she has constrained what information she is presented with and rationalized what she did get told. JT took a more hostile approach than JS but the outcome of her sensemaking is the same – reinforced thinking and process change delegated to leaders below her. Her phrase that 'you keep telling me there are problems but you don't solve them' seems like an abdication of leadership and runs counter to the principles of the methodology that the senior leaders role is to solve problems. My sense was that JT's lack of engagement meant that the change in mindset she was being asked to embrace would have created too much dissonance because we had failed to gain her commitment compliance at the outset and we were witnessing her consequent rationalization and defensiveness.

Note

1 NIMBY – 'not in my back yard'. A phrase commonly used in planning applications to describe people who accept the need for a development but oppose it in their own locality.

References

Aronson, E. 1992. The return of the repressed: Dissonance theory makes a comeback. *Psychological Inquiry*, Vol. 3, 303–311.

Aronson, E. 1997. Review: Back to the future: Retrospective review of Leon Festinger's "a theory of cognitive dissonance". *The American Journal of Psychology*, Vols. 110–137, 127.

Bacharach, S. B., Bamberger, P. & Sonnenstuhl, W. J. 1996. The organizational transformation process: The micropolitics of dissonance reduction and the alignment of logics of action. *Administrative Science Quarterly*, Vol. 41, 477–506.

Beauvois, J.-L. & Joule, R.-V. 1996. *A Radical Dissonance Theory*, London, Taylor and Francis.

Beauvois, J.-L. & Joule, R.-V. 1999. A radical point of view on dissonance theory. *In:* Mills, E. H.-J. J. (ed.) *Cognitive Dissonance: progress on a pivotal theory in social psychology*. (pp. 51–74). Washington, DC: American Psychological Association.

Festinger, L. 1957. *A Theory of Cognitive Dissonance*, Stanford, Stanford University Press.

Harmon-Jones, E. & Mills, J. (eds.) 1999. *Cognitive Dissonance: Progess on a Pivotal Theory in Social Psychology*, Washington: American Psychological Association.

10 Defensive Reasoning

Rationalizing Not Rational

In Chapter 8 I talked about the small group of leaders I worked with to create a war room in which we presented a slide demonstrating a top-heavy leadership structure. It had taken a long time to get what I had assumed would be simple information from Departmental leaders and I talked to my fellow leaders on the intervention group about this:

DD: The reason it took so long [to get the data] is the games that were being played.
Me: what do you mean?
AW: well for a start there's the [uses fingers to indicate 'quotes'] 'reduction' in IT staff employed in departments. Before you started the CE said that they [departments] weren't to have their own IT staff and so they had to get rid of them, which they did and so the CE was happy. But when we go in to do this count up [staff/mgt count] what do we find? Sure enough no IT people ... but a bunch of 'business analysts'. They'd just redesignated them. Departments will deny they're IT people of course.
Me: call me naïve, but didn't HR or the Chief Exec figure out what was happening? How did they get away with it?
DD: who knew and who was going to tell them?
AW: – look, I'm not saying this happens ... it doesn't ... but it happens, if you know what I'm saying (winks).

The other two leaders present (DD and BB) nodded but said nothing. It seemed to me that they knew exactly what AW was saying. It went unquestioned, no words of acknowledgement were needed that we were talking about things that happen, that everyone knows happens, but that no one will openly admit happens. Officially they don't happen. As leaders we state that they don't happen. And even though we know they do happen, we never say so directly. In my research diary that day I wrote:

> Well that was astonishing 'I'm not saying it happens, it doesn't, but it happens, if you know what I'm saying'. If I remember rightly that

> is almost exactly what Argyris says about defensive reasoning. Understanding this defensive reasoning is crucial if we are going to move leaders from single loop to double loop learning. I really wonder if raising this example will affect the wider leader group reaction to the war room? And how much of the rest of the data is 'unsayable'? The point of [the methodology] is that we get leaders to surface their defensive reasoning themselves because they need to see it for themselves. But we're going to be hitting them with it when they walk in the room and I'm not sure they'll take too well to it. But maybe it'll be the shock to the system they need.

AW's description of what was happening does indeed seem very close to Argyris's (1976, 1980, 1990, 1993, 2004) concept of defensive reasoning. Argyris seeks to explain why people indulge in such behavior when he argues that:

> Human beings seek to be in command of their actions. They feel good when they are able to produce the consequences that they intend. They abhor feeling or being out of control … [they] have programs in their heads about how to be in control, especially when they face embarrassment or threat.
>
> (Argyris, 1990, p.12)

He goes on to argue that these programs can be observed in two forms. First there are the beliefs and values (rules) that people hold about how to manage their lives, what he calls 'espoused theories of action'. Second, there are the actual rules that people exhibit in their behaviors, what he calls 'theories-in-use' (Argyris, 1990, p.13). He goes on to argue that theories in use often fall into what he calls Model 1 in which individuals engage in a strategy of winning but without making the other party lose face. In practice this leads to the sort of game playing and paradoxical behavior described by AW:

> … participants know they are playing games whose rules are: I know that I am and you are covering up. You know the same about me. Both of us know that we will not make what we know discussable. Both of us know that we will act as if we are not playing this game.
>
> (Argyris, 2004, p.67)

This fits with BB's earlier sensemaking conclusion in Chapter 8 that the wider leadership group members were not necessarily Machiavellian, rather their defensive routine behaviors may be their 'antidote to the organization'. So the challenge for our small group of leaders was going to be finding a way of saying the unsayable in the war room and as I explained in Chapter 8, we failed miserably.

I spoke to one of the leaders who had visited the war room and rationalized what she had seen in what she called the pyramid slide (the picture of a top-heavy leadership structure):

Me: we spent a lot of time gathering that data and it was the managers in the relevant departments or HR or Finance that gave us it, but you said you felt it's not accurate. Can I ask what you are not happy about?

HE: I know the team spent a lot of time getting the data and I don't want them thinking I was having a go at them. But when I saw that pyramid slide I got quite upset because there's been a lot of noise as a strategy by some leaders about cutting other people's departments as a way of deflecting the pressure on their own [departments]. I looked at that slide and I thought this is just the ammunition they need for a bun fight. And it's central [support] departments like mine that will be under attack most. And then there's all the other people that will seize it for their own agendas.

Me: what do you mean?

HE: the unions. They'll love it and say oh it's easy then just make a load of leaders redundant and problem solved.

Me: yeah I understand that the data is sensitive. What we tried to present in the war room was a holistic picture of [organization] and the interconnections between all the elements and thinking that led to them. There's no silver bullet and I understand that's a danger if any of the data is taken in isolation or out of context.

HE: well it will be I can guarantee that, which is why you can't present it that way and that's why I got angry when I saw it. I mean we know there's too many leaders but we've got to be careful about saying it. Any solution will end up with less leaders anyway so there's no need to emphasize it in the data.

Me: Well to be honest I'm not sure that the solution is just a pro-rata reduction in leaders under some sort of salami-slicing solution that we've used in the past. Perhaps mgt/support needs to take a proportionately bigger hit if we're going to protect services as much as we can, and that means we need to think very differently about how we design and run [organization].

HE: yes I get that but we need to work out what the new structures are *before* we start talking about the frontline/mgt split.

Me: ok but how are we going to get leaders buying into a radical restructure if they don't accept there's a problem in the first place.

HE: they all know there's a problem but you won't get them sorting it by making it public.

Me: don't lift the rock to see what's underneath? (laughs).

HE: lift it, but not when anyone else is looking (laughs).

HE was following a defensive reasoning approach which seemed to me to be a result of feeling threatened. It turns out her questioning of the data was not because it was wrong but because it was saying the unsayable. Challenging the data or the way it was calculated was therefore a way of unsaying the unsayable that had just been said (putting it back under the rock we'd turned over). The idea that we could come up with a solution that would deal with the problem when we weren't prepared to acknowledge or talk about it might seem irrational to an impartial observer, but it was effective rationalizing of the issue to HE.

As I explained at the start of the book, I was an active participant in all the research organizations and I have tried to illustrate that I was always part of the social sensemaking that was taking place. This is well demonstrated in an example of when I was part of a group of leaders that took some time out to make sense of how an intervention was going. We brought in an external facilitator to help us do this and the outcome was a lesson in how we ourselves were engaging in defensive reasoning (and also demonstrated the interconnectivity of sensemaking elements).

The facilitator asked us each to give a summary of progress to date and there was evidence of a developing sensemaking story trope of attribution of responsibility – with us as the heroes of new thinking battling the forces of the ignorant old world thinking leaders. The facilitator then asked how we thought our thinking differed from that of the other leaders:

Leader 1: It depends on the definition of transformation, you need the right people leading it and the right people engaged with rigor, talent, ambition and, to some extent, being able to cope with a degree of uncertainty, you know, that in three years' time none of us know where we're going to be. But I wouldn't batten down the hatches like them and say, oh I have to protect my department, you know, to the nth degree, because I think actually you marginalize yourself so much actually that if you're not in the tent opening your mind you're on a hiding to nothing, would be my view.

Leader 2: So we're trying to break down that culture. And also, we need people who are prepared to be interchangeable and to be prepared to not be precious about their own status or, you know, domain and all the rest of it.

Leader 3: It's so frustrating and depressing being asked to do stuff you know is worse for the organization. I would just give up if I could afford to but I can't. I used to work the old way and I thought it was best so I know where they are coming from. But I've tried to tell them about what we've done and they're just not willing to listen. It feels like I'm an outsider now and the only way to get back in is by working the old way.

Trouble is I now know how wrong that is so I'll be unhappy in my work.

Our sensemaking was similar to the sensemaking stories I had heard from the leaders in Chapter 3. The attribution of responsibility and unity was there, we were heroically persisting in the face of collective ignorance and self-interest. But it seemed to have reached a turning point with talk about leaving the organization. Leader 3 expresses a sense of our alienation from the other leaders when using the phrase 'I used to work the old way and I thought it was best. I feel like I'm an outsider now'. Our mindset had moved from the 'old way' and as a group we were frustrated that the others were still located in this old way of thinking. This is similar to the stories of leaders in Chapter 3 who said that once you have knowledge you can't go back to ignorance.

However, the facilitator went on to challenge us to reflect on our stories and probed why other leaders were not responding to our attempts to 'educate' them:

Leader 1: So we haven't got the message over effectively and it was a big stumbling block when it came to leaders making sense of what we proposed. They obviously try to do this from their current perspective and from that perspective they can fairly easily say 'we know all of this already so why do we need to change our thinking' even though they clearly didn't know most of it. We haven't got this message over effectively and looking back I can see that we haven't talked about it or illustrated it as much as perhaps we should have.

Leader 2: Maybe we didn't model the thinking we wanted from them so they thought we were saying one thing but doing another. I'm not sure we were as brave as we were asking them to be. For example when I'm meeting [Chief Executive] and I'm thinking about a staircase of bravery or actually maybe a diving board at the swimming pool. Do I dive off the 15m or 2m board? My sense is that I need to be on the 15m board in terms of honesty about what's happening and what he needs to do. But I need to know that he's on the 15m board with me. If he's not, I'll climb down to the 2m board he's on!

The facilitator had managed to get us to reflect on our sensemaking stories and develop them by saying our own unsayables. The facilitated session lasted 8 hours and there were many more similar discussions as we reflected further. We had moved from heroes blaming other leaders for their failure to engage with the methodology to accepting that perhaps we had a role as villains in this story. The example above brings out some important issues that shaped our ongoing sensemaking that day:

1. An admission that the way we had gone about things contributed to our failure to engage other leaders. It felt to me at this session that the facilitator was engaging us in the same process of reflexive practice that we ourselves had failed to get other leaders to engage in. This reflexive practice helped us produce new thinking and insights into what had happened and it felt like we were beginning to acknowledge our own defensive reasoning.
2. We had allowed ourselves to mirror other leader thinking rather than model the new thinking and leader 2's point about standing of the 2m or 15m platform sums up our reaction to the frustration we were feeling at the lack of progress, so if ever there was a time for us to climb to the 15m board that had been it. But we were feeling uncomfortable doing that and knew we would stay on the 2m board along with the CE. In our social sensemaking the facilitator was helping us to see that while it might make a good story about our bravado of positioning ourselves on the 15m board, our theory in action was staying on the 2m board.

Another common example of defensive reasoning in organizations concerns expensive shiny new IT systems that fail to deliver their expected benefits. This is a rich ground for observing the collective social nature of defensive reasoning as this typical exchange illustrates:

HT: everyone knows that [IT System] doesn't work so there's nothing really new in that although the data makes it much clearer. But it's better than nothing - we are where we are and you can't change history. So the issue becomes how do we make it work? Board are never going to put their hands up and say they made a bad decision, they want to hear how we're going to make things better.

HT's reaction to the data contains a number of sensemaking elements. There is preunderstanding when she says that everyone knows the IT system doesn't work. Notwithstanding that everyone knows the IT system does not work, HT goes on to say that the Board will never admit it is a bad decision. She is articulating defensive reasoning in the organization, i.e. organizational leaders know the IT was a bad decision, but it must never be admitted that it was a bad decision and leaders must act in a way that covers up the fact that they know it was a bad decision. This cover up includes forcing business areas to use the IT and find ways of making it work so that the cover up remains covered up (even though everyone knows it's a cover up). My assumption had been that because HT had not been involved in the original decision that she would be willing to confront the issue. But I had made the mistake of thinking of HT's sensemaking as an individual activity when actually sensemaking is a social activity and failed to recognize that the collective rationalizing of a 'bad' decision not only included those who were involved in the original decision but had, via defensive reasoning, been passed on to, and embraced by, subsequent leaders such as HT and encapsulated in her phrase 'you can't change history'.

Another frequent example of defensive reasoning by leaders in their early stages of engagement with the methodologies relates to the impact of the functional silos found in most organizations. In most cases the design of their business units was demonstrated to have significant negative impacts on performance. This finding was counterintuitive to the leaders I was working with as they had considerable pre-understanding that functionalization is an effective way to design and lead organizations. After studying his area of the business one leader (JC) gave a response that was typical of most leaders I worked with in the research. The systems picture that JC had worked with his team to develop clearly demonstrated that one of the major constraints on organizational performance and customer service was the significant degree of functionalization within his business area. His sensemaking of this was articulated in a reflexive practice session with his team which I facilitated:

JC: Ok I get that the functions we've created are getting in the way and causing a lot of the problems that we've seen. I think we can all see that and are agreed on it. But the issue is what's the alternative? There's no organization in the world that has gotten rid of their functions and just have one big team where everybody does everything! Businesses can't work that way and functions are there because it's the most effective and efficient way to run [the business] ... so we're stuck with that aspect and there's no point going to [Chief Executive] and saying everything you know about how to build your organization is wrong! It's just a reality we've got to accept and mitigate the worst bits of it.

Me: I've worked in and been a leader in organizations that have swept away a lot of functionalization. I've led a business area in which HR and IT and so on weren't functions but were people located in my business and providing support in the business ... we were just one big team but it didn't mean everybody had to be able to do everything. There *are* alternatives to functionalization that retain specialisms.

JC: (paused to think about what I'd said) ... ok I'm sure that's true but I'm pretty sure it wasn't in our line of business? I'm sure there are small organizations or the 'creative' industries that can play about with different structures but it would never work in something as complex as our business ... and anyway even if it could [the senior leaders] would never buy it. They're proud of our 300-year history ...

Me: yeah but they've also stated they want us to become the 300-year-old industry disruptor ....

JC: ok well you tell me how we can make this work in one big team ...

Me: It's not for me to suggest any solutions, my role is to help you put aside our current thinking about how we design the business and challenge ourselves about alternatives. Maybe our current structure is the best option, I don't know ... but we know the cost and bad customer service it's driving into the business ... so the question is 'if we had a blank sheet of paper and were starting afresh, is this how we'd design the business? ...'

JC: ok I'm up for that because I don't think it is, obviously knowing what we know now, but I was just sounding a note of caution that there's a lot of vested interests in the current structures and we'll have a lot of leaders trying to rubbish anything different that we come up with.

My interpretation of JC's sensemaking at this point is that it demonstrates two common lines of defensive reasoning that were typical of leaders in all the research organizations.

The first line of defensive reasoning illustrated in JC's first comment is a curious mix of compresence of opposites, preunderstanding, storytelling trope of attribution of responsibility, and a sense of fatalism – that there is nothing we can do about it and it is almost ridiculous to suggest otherwise. On the one hand JC admits that functionalization is a significant cause of organizational problems but in the same breath adds that it is the most effective and efficient way to lead an organization. His preunderstanding is that all leaders and organizations think this way and there are no alternative organizational designs. Notwithstanding that he thinks functionalization is the most effective and efficient way to design an organization he then says we are 'stuck' with it and, in an example of a sensemaking story trope of attribution of responsibility, points blame in the direction of the Chief Executive who he implies is the architect of this thinking. This then leads to his fatalistic sensemaking that the Chief Executive will not be prepared to listen to, or accept, alternatives to the current organizational design model. His sensemaking is common of leaders in the research in that it is self-fulfilling. The Chief Executive will not countenance alternatives so there is no point wasting time suggesting them. The Chief Executive is never challenged to consider alternatives and the continuation of the status quo is then deemed to be both proof that he would not change his thinking and also allows him to be painted as the villain of the story.

I sought to challenge JC's preunderstanding by offering examples of leaders and organizations that had found alternatives to the levels of functionalization identified as a problem in this research organization. JC responded to this with the second line of defensive reasoning, which was very common among leaders in the research (and linked to the commitment compliance sensemaking element in Chapter 9) and was a 'but we're different' argument. JC's sensemaking moved on to accept that there may indeed be alternatives but defended against this by arguing that they would not be appropriate for the particular nature of his business. Most the leaders I coached in the research organizations engaged in this line of reasoning. They sought to find ways in which their business area was different and not suitable for alternatives that may have worked in other areas. JC's thinking moved from all organizations use functionalization, to only small or creative industry organizations are able to move away from functionalization, although he did so without any supporting evidence to back this up. As LB, a leader in the housing organization engaged in this research, said of his experience of leader sensemaking: 'a leader's best defense [against the methodology] is to damn it with faint praise and adopt the "do it to them, not me" strategy'.

However, I do not interpret JC's defensive reasoning to be resistance to change. Theories of cognitive dissonance, organizational defensive reasoning, displacement of concepts, sensemaking and preunderstanding all propose that such rationalization is to be expected in situations which challenge leaders' current mindsets. It is an inevitable reaction to data that challenge existing perceptions.

By gaining leader compliance commitment I was able to engage them in reflexive practice which in many cases allowed them to recognize their defensive reasoning and move to a questioning of their current mindsets. The degree of initial rationalization varied between leaders in the initial stages of engagement and some moved on more quickly than others. The methodologies I used recognize that initial rationalizing of what they find is a predictable outcome of the cognitive dissonance experienced by leaders as they engage in their commitment compliance. The solution is to engage leaders in reflexive practice that reveals strategic problems and issues caused directly by current leader mindsets and which engages leaders in exploring alternative ways of thinking about leading and organizing.

References

Argyris, C. 1976. Single-loop and double-loop models in research on decision making. *Administrative Science Quarterly*, Vol. 21, 363–375.

Argyris, C. 1980. Making the undiscussable and its undiscussability discussable. *Public Administration Review*, Vol. 40, 205–213.

Argyris, C. 1990. *Overcoming Organizational Defenses: Facilitating Organizational Learning*, Boston, Allyn and Bacon.

Argyris, C. 1993. *Knowledge for Action: A Guide to Overcoming Barriers to Organizational Change*, San Fransisco, Jossey-Bass.

Argyris, C. 2004. *Reasons and Rationalizations: The Limits to Organizational Knowledge*, Oxford, Oxford University Press.

11 Compresence of Opposites

And Makes More Sense than *or*

Heraclitus in the second-century BC proposed the harmony of opposites in which he suggests that things can contain opposite qualities. Ancient Chinese Daoist philosophy also contains the concept of a combined Yin and Yang of equal and opposite qualities. What prevents this line of thought being criticized as logical fallacy is that Heraclitus and Daoism were not suggesting that the qualities exist at the same time, rather that they are complementary and transform each other. Heraclitus was arguing that it is a combination of opposites that give a thing its existence:

> Contrary qualities are found in us … but they are the same by virtue of one thing changing around to another. We are asleep and we wake up; we are awake and we go to sleep. Thus sleep and waking are both found in us, but not at the same time or in the same respect. Contraries are the same by virtue of constituting a system of connections: alive-dead, waking-sleeping, young-old. Subjects do not possess incompatible properties at the same time, but at different times.
>
> (Graham, 2015)

So what has this got to do with leader sensemaking of organizational change? My research found that not only does sensemaking embrace a harmony of opposites, but it goes further and embraces a compresence of opposites which is the state of opposites being present together at the same time as captured in the opening lines of the Dickens classic:

> 'It was the best of times, it was the worst of times, it was the age of wisdom, it was the age of foolishness, it was the epoch of belief, it was the epoch of incredulity …'
>
> (Dickens, 1859, p.5)

In Dickens' first lines from A Tale of Two Cities his compresence of opposites presents the readers with a paradox. How can it be both the best and worst of times at the same time? The sensemaking stories of the leaders I interviewed in Chapter 3 seemed to present a similar paradox – the change of thinking was fast, the change of thinking was slow. How could their sensemaking embrace the oxymoron of a slow, fast changes in thinking? Clues can be seen in the ontology (Chapter 4) and displacement of concepts (Chapter 6) elements of sensemaking. If, as the leaders did in these chapters, we can hold multiple realities and multiple concepts then it is not such a huge step to sensing that we can experience opposites at the same time. In fact most of us will experience a compresence of opposites at some point. I asked you at the start of the book whether you believed the Earth revolves around the Sun or the other way round. By now you will know that your answer is linked to your ontological perspective and your preunderstanding. Most people believe that it is the Earth that revolves around the Sun and know this to be true from second-hand pre-understanding. But their lived experience is of a Sun that moves, not the Earth. Why else do we talk of the Sun rising in the morning and setting in the evening after its journey across the sky? Or what about pain and pleasure? Most people think of these as a harmony of opposites in which we will experience both but at different times although for some people sexual pleasure is only achieved when experiencing pain at the same time. There is a popular internet meme with people asking why they are so stressed *and* bored? Most of us will at some time have experienced morbid fascination when something irresistibly attracts our interest while repulsing us at the same time. The compresence of opposites is the ability in our sensemaking to experience opposites at the same time – it replaces 'or' with 'and'.

What I found in my research is that leader sensemaking embraces not only a harmony of opposites in which opposites are experienced at different times but can sometimes embrace a compresence of opposites in which opposites are sensed as being experienced at the same time. It may be a logical fallacy, but it seems to help leaders with their sensemaking.

A common example I came across with leaders in all organizations was their sensing of the concept of speed. Leaders in the early stages of engaging with the change methodologies felt a confusing sense of it being both slow and fast at the same time. At first I interpreted this as simply being retrospective sensemaking in which they felt it to be slow during the early stages of data gathering but later after some reflection they decided it had actually been fast – a harmony of opposites. However, the more I worked with leaders the more that my own sensemaking became that they were sensing a simultaneous compresence of speed and slowness. A typical example of conversations was a discussion I had with RM:

Me: I just want to touch base with you about how you are feeling about the intervention. I know its early days and we're only a couple of weeks in but I'm interested what you're making of it?

RM: hmm... mixed emotions is probably the honest answer (laughs)

Me: oh ok ... can I ask what the emotions are?

RM: well it's kind of ... let me think how to put it ... it's difficult to express my thoughts properly ... I know it's only been a couple of weeks and actually we've revealed so much already but it also feels like ... sort of we've been doing it for months! I get that we've got to be thorough and wouldn't want not to be but at the same time I think we're all beginning to think kind of when will it end? Do you know what I mean? I think we've made fantastic progress and already we've got some great insights in just a couple of weeks but at the same time if feels like we're wading through porridge (laughs). Does it always feel like this when you're doing it [methodology]?

RM was thinking out loud and trying to sensemake in the moment. She was struggling with the quick results that had already been achieved but was trying to reconcile this with a sense of it being a long haul. She was experiencing the two opposite feelings and this explains her sense of confusion. It is a very common reaction from leaders in the early days of engagement with the methodologies, but sense of speed is not the only example. Another common compresence of opposites was leader sensemaking of interventions as being both easy and difficult. The basic approach in all the methodologies was similar – leader involvement in action research and reflection which involves gathering data about the organization structure and design, customers and their demands, and organizational performance. A common reaction from leaders when they first had the methodology explained to them was that it seemed quite simple and was often called 'just common sense'. However, as leaders engaged in the action research they often struggled and found it difficult to gather data that they felt should be easy to collect. I had similar conversations to the one with RM regarding speed. One leader expressed compresence of opposites succinctly:

WJ: look this is easy as piss ... it's not rocket science but it's turned into a nightmare ... I just don't get how something so easy as getting customer volumes can be so [expletive] difficult!

Is It Compresence or Is It Harmony?

The sensemaking stories of leaders develop as a continuous stream and contain a mix of opposites. In some cases the mix of opposites is Heraclitan or Daoist in the sense that leaders retrospectively construct stories in which the opposites are reconciled. In the sensemaking stories of the leaders in Chapter 3 we saw this when they first described their almost immediate ah-ha! moments of insight but when pushed conceded that actually it took up to two years for them fully to get it. We will see the same retrospective reconciling of opposites in the post-engagement stories of leaders in Chapter 13.

But sometimes leaders seem to embrace opposites in the moment. This is a logical fallacy if our current orthodoxy is that opposites are two ends of a continuum and are 'either/or'. An intervention can only be slow 'or' fast, it cannot be both at the same time. It may move from one to another and back but at any given point it must fall at just one point on the continuum. Notwithstanding current orthodoxy, leader sensemaking has shown the ability to move beyond the confines of 'or' and in which opposites may represent two ends of a continuum but that at any given moment two, or more, points may co-exist. This alternative orthodoxy moves from 'or' to 'and'.

This element is in some ways the most counterintuitive element of sensemaking for leaders as they engage with the methodology and interventionists need to understand and address this in reflexive practice with leaders. Moving from a modern to postmodern perspective is counterintuitive to leaders who have spent many years developing their modernist approach. Combined with all the other elements of sensemaking it leads to many apparent paradoxes and compresence of opposites in leader sensemaking. Interventionists need to understand that the 'logical fallacy' of compresence of opposites is no less real in sensemaking than displaced concepts that embrace different paradigms or modernist leaders who are comfortable with multiple realities. The compresence of opposites is not something that interventionists should be trying to get leaders to avoid but rather to be actively encouraged as an aid to sensemaking that leads to mindset change.

References

Dickens, C. 1859. *A Tale of Two Cities*, London, Penguin Books.

Graham, D. W. 2015. Heraclitus. In: Zalta, E. N. (ed.) The Stanford Encyclopedia of Philosophy. Online.

12 Interpretation

Decide First, Justify Later

When, at the start of this section of the book, I asked you whether the Earth is round or flat I set the boundaries of the issue I wanted you to make sense of. In other words I generated what I wanted you to make sense of. I limited your options to a round or flat Earth, but there are countless other options in terms of possible shapes or even premises that the Earth is shapeless or there is no such thing as the Earth. My use of 'or' also discouraged sensemaking of a compresence of opposites that the Earth is both flat *and* round. Having set the boundaries I then used your possible answers in subsequent Chapters to interpret your sensemaking based on this limited choice of options.

Interpretation is the last sensemaking element that I explain in this book, but as I explained previously, there is no linear sequence of sensemaking elements and interpretation will be evident throughout leaders sensemaking. It can be seen happening in all the previous chapters and will be very evident in Section 3 of the book when I observe a global post-engagement social sensemaking event.

It might seem that sensemaking and interpretation are synonyms for the process of understanding something. Weick, however, is clear that they are quite distinct concepts and that an understanding of sensemaking also requires being clear about what it is not. And it is not interpretation. Although interpretation is an element of sensemaking, sensemaking is about how people generate that which they then interpret. Sensemaking therefore precedes, determines and follows interpretation.

> Schon (1983) uses the example of problem setting to highlight the separation of sensemaking and interpretation. Whilst setting the boundaries of a problem is an essential part of problem solving, it in itself creates the problem. Schon argues that we need to recognize that: ... when we set the problem, we select what we will treat as the "things" of the situation, we set the boundaries of our attention to it, and we impose upon it a coherence which allows us to say what is wrong and in what directions the situation needs to be changed.
>
> (Schon, 1983, p.40)

In other words, sensemaking involves selecting one out of a myriad of possible interpretations of what is being experienced and using one of a myriad of possible explanations to make sense of our chosen interpretation. One important outcome of this continuous circular process of sensemaking and interpretation is that:

> ... it leads to justifications for past and future actions. Once a commitment to action is made, the process of providing an explanation for a particular interpretation simultaneously creates justifications for past events and future courses of action. Creating these justifications is not a one-time event in sensemaking, but an ongoing process whereby the justifications shapes actions and then those actions shape further justifications.
>
> (Kramer, 2017)

In chapter 9 a leader interpreted my use of the word 'necessary' as being me asking him to commit to full-time engagement. Throughout Chapters 3–11 intervention leaders interpreted other leaders not responding positively to attempts to get their engagement with the methodology as deliberate resistance. However, we saw in Chapter 10 that reflexive practice led the small group of intervention leaders responsible for the war room to reinterpret their story of a heroic fight in the face of fierce resistance to one of our failure to use the right approach to get their engagement.

Another example of interpretation as part of sensemaking was a group of leaders in one of the research organizations who took time out to reflect on progress in a transformation intervention they were supporting. We gathered at a leadership away day which was an off-site event run to allow us to interpret what had happened so far – justification for past actions and to shape future actions. The first activity at the away day was for each of us capture our thoughts about the current state of our intervention in the form of a visual metaphor. The graphics that were produced are examples of the power of metaphor in helping individuals interpret their reality and construct their stories:

> Leader 1 drew a picture of a snow globe with an elephant floating freely in the liquid so that whatever way you turned the globe the elephant stayed upright. He explained that wider leadership is the elephant and no matter what we do they never change and keep on doing things the way they've always done them. He finished by saying that 'maybe I just have to accept that I work in an organization that does not want to change and can't be made to'
>
> Leader 2 pictured a bath filled with cold water and the transformation methodology as a cup of hot water being poured into it. His sense was that you can't heat a bath of cold water with a cup of hot

water – it's the other way around. Trying to convince wider leadership of the methodology made him feel like the cup of hot water and he was scared the experience would cool him down, meaning he worried about reverting to the old way of thinking. Scattered around the outside of the bath was a pack of playing cards. The cards represented the game playing that was going on as part of the wider leadership response to the methodology.

Leader 3 had drawn a picture of him engaged in a Sisyphean task of rolling a huge boulder up a hill, except that the hillside was a series of steps rather than an even slope. He explained that 'it started as a straight line but then I decided it's actually more like a series of steps. There has to be some willingness to change. It needs strong leadership that say 'look it's going to happen and you've got no choice'. But he felt that we spent more time going backwards than forwards – one step change forward and two back. We were trying to push the wider leadership up the hill but it will never work and they will keep rolling back down the hill. The wider leadership need to decide if they want to climb the hill, we can't push them up it.

Leader 4 presented a picture of a snakes and ladder board. He felt that the whole experience of working with the wider leadership had been like a game of snakes and ladders but with a lot more snakes than ladders and with the dice loaded against the methodology. It shared the sense of Leader 3's feeling of moving back more often than we move forward. The loaded dice represented the game playing of the wider leadership.

Leader 5 (me) presented a picture with an image of a rocket flying a few feet of the ground and following the path of a road which was heading towards a fork to left and right. The rocket was heading towards the right-hand fork which led to a crash into a brick wall. The left-hand fork led to a black hole. The wall represented continuing to lead the way we've always led and ending in disaster, whereas the black hole is the scariness and uncertainty of the methodology because we don't know what the new world will look like. My frustration is that the rocket is traveling at a snail's pace and we've seen the fork coming for a long time but the wider leadership are more scared of the uncertainty of the black hole than the certain destruction of brick wall and are refusing to change direction.

The group agreed that these were valid metaphorical interpretations of what was happening. As well as being strong metaphors for the sense-making journeys of the participants it is also interesting that they have similar storytelling tropes of attribution of responsibility and unity as used in the stories of the leaders interviewed in Chapter 3. The leaders in Chapter 3 told me how, with persistence, they had successfully overcome the ignorance and resistance of others. The sensemaking stories of the leaders at this away day were about frustration at failure to properly engage other leaders at this stage of the intervention but already a shared story of heroic persistence in the face of ignorance and resistance to change by others was beginning to emerge.

Our interpretations were of resistance to the methodology because of:

- Fear of the unknown
- Game playing
- Lack of leadership
- Restraining forces pulling leaders back to 'old world' thinking

The next step was to shape future actions based on these interpretations. Having learned from previous interventions, the answer lay not in building a heroic story of failure in the face of overwhelming odds but rather questioning what it was we were doing that was either causing the reactions or what it was we could do to respond them. Fear of the unknown seemed like something that was directly in our gift to respond to and seemed to arise from lack of clarity about how the methodology worked and what outcomes might be. This led to us reviewing our communication strategy. Game playing was a more endemic cultural issue and linked to defensive reasoning which we felt needed to be tackled in conjunction with efforts to get the Chief Executive more actively owning and leading the intervention. The restraining forces are an ever-present threat to mindset change and in our case we spent more time focusing on specifically what aspects of current leadership orthodoxy were acting as restraining forces and worked with the Chief Executive to counter these (one of the biggest restraining forces was the budget system and so making changes to this became one of our priorities). What is important for understanding sensemaking is not the specific actions we took but rather that we understood the need to constantly be challenging our own interpretations and trying to understand the interpretations of those we were trying to influence. Categorizing everything as 'resistance' is no way to influence those who have different interpretations from our own.

An interesting example of interpretation by leaders in a large financial services organization took place during a meeting I observed of senior leaders which was held to review progress on change initiatives within the business. The meeting was the culmination of several weeks work and was to be a dry run of a presentation the following week to key stakeholders including board members and heads of directorates. The topic was a summary of results achieved in delivering against plan in the previous quarter and plans for the upcoming quarter. As senior leaders from each of the business areas presented their slides there was increasing unease in the room about the obvious difference between what had been planned in the last quarter and what had actually been delivered. The consequence of this failure to deliver was that plans for the upcoming quarter were likely to be severely impacted by having to carry forward work that had not been completed in the previous quarter.

This in itself would have been a cause for concern but the bigger problem was that reporting during the quarter had been positive about hitting the planned outcomes and it was only now becoming apparent that at best leaders in certain areas had been hopelessly optimistic about their ability to deliver the outcomes or at worst had been hiding the reality that there was no possibility of them delivering the outcomes. I have found that this reporting upwards of good news about progress, even when it is obvious that progress is definitely not good, is done in the (often desperate) hope that the situation can somehow be recovered and is commonplace in organizations. As one leader in this organization told me on a separate occasion:

FG: we've got RAG [red/amber/green reporting on progress and risk of missing deadlines] reports coming out our ears but I don't know why because it's always a case of green, green, green ... until due date and then all of a sudden it's red with sort of 'oh we were blocked two months ago' or weren't given enough resource' or whatever. I mean, seriously, it's always the same – make out everything's ok and hide the fact you don't have a snowballs chance in hell of delivering until it's too late.

Me: what do you think stops people flagging things as red as soon as it's obvious that's what they are?

FR: hmm ... well fear probably. No one wants a kicking for delivering bad news so it's easier to keep them up above happy until the last moment because you never know, you might actually sort something out and then you wouldn't have needed the kicking in the first place. And since everyone's doing it you've got less chance of being shot putting your head above the parapet when everyone else is admitting it than if you do it on your own earlier

These mixed metaphors seem like another example of defensive reasoning in action in that everyone knows the rules of this game and of course normally no one would ever admit it. However, the meeting of leaders had almost surfaced this unsayable and the leaders had to interpret the situation in a way that kept the unsayable unsaid, i.e. justify past actions and plan future actions:

Leader 1: well we clearly haven't delivered on what we said we would and a lot of stuff is going to have to be taken forward. It's not good but we can position it carefully as 'it could have been a lot worse given all the headwinds we've had [name various internal and external crises/calamities that affected the business]'

Leader 2: We've delivered a lot even in the [projects] we haven't completed so we've still achieved significant portions so we could break them down into smaller projects that we've delivered and the rest are future projects?

Leader 3: hmm ... but that's going to have a major impact on the next quarter plans that we've produced [which were produced on the belief that everything was 'green']. The stakeholders are never going to wear this if we say we couldn't complete everything this quarter but we're going to complete it all next quarter *as well* as everything we have planned for next quarter. They'll rip it to shreds

Leader 1: I agree and we're not going to sort this out in time for the meeting next week. I think we have to cancel next week's meeting and move it a month to give us time to see what the actual picture is on this quarter and work out that it means on the plans for next quarter

Leader 4: They're not going to be happy. We've told them months ago they have to clear their diaries for the meeting next week because it's an immoveable feast and now a few days to go and we just postpone it?

Leader 1: We can blame it on time and diary constraints

Leader 3: Or we could even tell the truth (everyone laughs)

All: Discussion about what 'constraints' are to be used to justify the postponement

Leader 3: Ok so we are saying to them that it's because of [lists constraints that have been agreed]

All: laughter

Leader 3: Why's everyone laughing?

Leader 2: We thought you were going to say 'Ok so we've agreed to tell the truth' again (everyone laughs)

It seems to me that the collective sensemaking interpretation of the leaders contained the following elements:

- That there be no discussion of why the problems were only evident now when they had obviously arisen some time ago
- The problem has been unforeseen headwinds that knocked plans off course
- We need time to come up with a credible explanation of the impact on the upcoming quarter and to replan based on what we identify will be carried forward into the next quarter
- Stakeholders will be very unhappy with the postponement of the meeting and so we need to come up with credible constraints that require it to be delayed (but not the 'truth')

This all appears very Machiavellian but in my experience is not an unusual example of interpretation in organizations and is understandable. In political life we have seen similar interpretations of 'questionable' behavior being described as being economical with the truth or of the use of alternative facts. The point is that interpretation, like storytelling or sensemaking as a whole, is about the selection of one possible interpretation from many possibilities. The one that is chosen will be the best fit for the overall sensemaking process and will be influenced by the other eight sensemaking elements. For an interventionist the important thing is to try as best as possible to understand the factors influencing chosen interpretations and to act on these factors if they wish leaders to actively consider alternative interpretations. In this case it seems that one issue causing defensive reasoning and therefore pointing leaders in the direction of their chosen interpretation is a culture of fear and of being given a 'kicking' if you are too honest. Without addressing this issue any interventionist will struggle to get leaders to seriously consider an interpretation that involves telling the 'truth'.

While interpretation is evident in all the elements of sensemaking it is particularly strong in the retrospective post-engagement sensemaking stories of leaders. We saw this in Chapter 3 and it will also be evident in the next Chapter as I describe a session I attended of leaders from across the globe as they interpreted and made sense of their experiences engaging with a transformation methodology.

References

Kramer, M. W. 2017. Sensemaking. *In*: Scott, C. R. & Lewis, L. K. (eds.) *The International Encyclopedia of Organizational Communication*. (pp. 1–10). New York: John Wiley & Sons.

Schon, D. A. 1983. *The Reflective Practitioner: How Professionals Think in Action*, London, Ashgate.

Part III

Post-Engagement Sensemaking Observed

In Part One I recounted the post-engagement sensemaking stories of leaders and identified some common elements. In Part Two I covered the nine elements of sensemaking I observed as leaders tried to make sense of transformational change initiatives. While some of the elements resonated with the post-engagement stories in Chapter 3 there were also some differences. The sensemaking was nothing like as linear or dramatic as the stories of leaders in Chapter 3 which were of successfully overcoming the forces of resistance, whereas in the research organizations the leaders sensemaking was less linear, much messier and attempts to gain commitment compliance met with mixed success. In Part Three I return to post-engagement sensemaking and listen to the stories of leaders who had emerged from their engagement with a transformation methodology with new thinking.

13 Post-Engagement Social Sensemaking

What Is History but a Fable Agreed upon

Towards the end of my research I was presented with an opportunity to observe a social sensemaking session for leaders that I had been working with in a global company. This was a meeting set up specifically to give leaders at Director level in business areas of the organization an opportunity to reflect on what they had learned from engaging with the methodology and to share this with leaders from other areas who were thinking about engaging with the methodology.

The meeting consisted of a series of facilitated sessions led by leaders who had engaged with, and were now advocates of, the methodology. Therefore, as with the leader stories in Chapter 3, it is missing the sensemaking stories of any leaders who engaged with the methodology but did not embrace, and were not advocates of, it. In the first session there was an interesting self-deprecating use of metaphors to joke about criticisms that are made of the methodology by leaders who either have not engaged with it or only know of it through second-hand preunderstanding:

Speaker 1: Good afternoon, I am [Name] ... or the Chief Jesuit Priest [audience laughter]. It's interesting that our [methodology advocate] leaders are known as religious zealots ... I'm not particularly a zealot about systems thinking but the thing that really really hacks me off is crappy customer service and crappy jobs that we give to our employees. So it's not a method thing it's more about a passion for our customer and our people.

My interpretation of this is that the leader has incorporated three important sensemaking themes in this short introduction:

1. He has used storytelling trope of unity. Leaders who have embraced the methodology are ridiculed by others as religious zealots because of their claims to being the only ones with knowledge and expertise. The others don't understand the true reality that the advocate leaders have discovered.

2. He has also used the storytelling trope of attribution of responsibility. The advocate leaders have acquired knowledge of reality and are now the heroes fighting 'crappy' customer service and employee working conditions, which non-advocate 'others' cannot see.
3. He also highlights that the methodology is not about method, it is about thinking – a passion for customer and employee. This is subtle but in my sensemaking he is saying that the methodology is not a modernist ontological 'project', it is a mindset change.

The leader went on to play a short video which demonstrated a customer receiving poor service and then asked leaders in the meeting to stand up:

> Everybody on your feet .... Remain standing if you think the case study we've just seen is a one-off and a really bad example or sit down if you think that kind of rubbish is endemic across our entire business. Everybody sat down (lots of laughter).

My sensemaking embraced two interpretations of this incident. First, I remember thinking at the time that this was a leading question and it would have taken a brave leader to remain standing. Given that the introduction described earlier set the scene for 'insiders' (advocates) and others, who would position themselves as an ignorant 'other'? However, after reflection on the entire meeting, I think that, notwithstanding there was an element of the question being leading, there was also an element of the collective leadership acknowledging a shift in mindset. These people, who had spent many years as leaders in the organization, were responsible for this endemic 'rubbish'. The methodology seeks to develop a new leadership mindset and confront the defensive reasoning that is a hallmark of leadership in organizations. This public and collective admission that the very system they had been responsible for was 'rubbish' seems like a significant saying of the unsayable and while it would have been uncomfortable for those who had not yet engaged with the methodology, it did open the way to make this particular unsayable, sayable.

Argyris disputes arguments that defensive routines are so embedded that they are unlikely to change and argues that 'research is needed that may provide new strategies that liberate us from defensive double binds' (Argyris, 2004, p. 68). Without overstating the case, I think that the 'leading question' exercise was a small example of liberation that a postmodern ontology could result in. Speaker 1 suggests this when he says that the rubbish service was caused by:

> .. the same management thinking, the same 200-year-old industrial thinking that we've used to create processes in our service industry. The thing I've learned, actually, after seeing our business around the

> world is that whilst yes national cultures are different, management thinking about the way we design service is the same, EVERYWHERE, because everyone's used this old, antiquated view of the [organizational] world.

There are two interesting points here. There is a statement that 200 years of thinking has led to and 'old' and 'antiquated' view of reality. In my reflective sensemaking, it seems metaphorically like the leader is saying something akin to those in history who challenged the widely held but antiquated view that the world was flat. It is a statement that the current mindset has to change. Secondly, the leader is making a point which reflects my own experience working with leaders around the globe that national cultures are not a significant factor in organizational sensemaking as modernist thinking is indeed endemic in leadership. Coincidentally, but as if to make that point, the leader from the French business was then invited to talk about his experience engaging with the methodology:

Speaker 2: Bonjour! Don't worry I won't be speaking in French! (laughter). [name] asked me to tell you my journey using the methodology in France.

> The first discussion I had with [leadership coaches] last spring, so probably one year ago, and my first reaction was ... well ... what is this methodology. First, it's a strange name, then its' 'not invented here'[France], worse 'invented in UK' (laughter), it's consultant stuff, and more than that, the French business is efficient .... We've been leading lots of efficiency projects, we've done lots of automations so why are we going to do this? But I must admit RW and HH are very good ambassadors for ST so we decided to have a try and start a [data gathering] phase on the business.

Once again, a brief introduction included some important sensemaking. The leader said that at the outset, the methodology, even the name, was strange. The leader didn't use the same phrases, but it seemed like he initially had the same view expressed by speaker 1's talk about people who see him as a religious zealot. The second element was a recognition of the modernist approach to change. At this first contact, the leader's reaction was we have already done lots of efficiency projects, we've done lots of automation projects, so why the need for this project. At that time the leader was good at 'doing' change and had implemented lots of projects and saw systems thinking as just another project. It is an acknowledgement of preunderstanding based on modernist thinking. He continues:

> And the result of the first data gathering phase is just this paper [unfurled a very long process flow map for the business on the floor of the meeting room some 20+ feet long] and my first reaction was well ... hmm ... shit that's probably not the best process we have (laughter) and at this stage you got be careful with the data you present to your employees and your managers because they share the same kind of reaction and you've got some people realizing they've been doing some work that is really not useful ... for weeks, for months and maybe for years and we've got even some people crying so you've got to explain that it's the system, it's not their work or the way they do their work, it is the system that has been designed not to be very efficient.

At the same time as telling his own sensemaking story the leader was also now beginning to talk about *giving* sense to employees. It seems to me that this move to thinking about how to give sense of the methodology to others suggests that he himself believes that he has fully engaged with the methodology. This engagement includes an understanding of the danger of the reaction to burning platform type events such as the war room example in Chapters 8 (or in his case the 20+ feet flow map). His description of people crying is an example of the powerful impact on people of their reality being challenged.

The leader's explanation to staff who were upset by the data was that it is the system, not them, that is to blame for the results. This seems like another acknowledgement of a change of mindset since a principle of the methodology is that the system is a result of leader thinking. Modernist organizations tend to link performance to people and the leader was recognizing that actually performance is largely determined by organizational design, not the people in the organization. This organizational heresy is significant. My own professional background is in HRM (the inappropriately named specialism of human resource management) and the very term 'human resource management' is indicative of modernist thinking in which organizational performance is a people (employee) issue. But here we have the leader of the business in France indicating a change in mindset and saying actually performance is a result of the design of the system, although he did leave it as implicit that the design of the system is a result of leadership mindset. He then explained to the meeting how, having engaged with the methodology he went about getting commitment compliance from his leadership team:

> We decided first – it's a cultural thing – to make it French, so the French thing was finding a French name and I think that was part of the success.
>
> Then you've got to bring your colleagues onboard, the other Executive Committee members and you first have to explain to

them what is .... We did some presentations and I brought all the EC members to the teams in order they could see all the papers, listen to customer calls, see all the failure in the process, organize a travel to [Head Office] to spend some time looking at other areas of the business [that had engaged with the methodology]. We also did some presentations to all the managers in France, the top management.

Notwithstanding that I have said there was no significant national cultural differences in my research findings, the leader does make the point that context can influence sensemaking and that the language used in the UK version of the methodology did not translate effectively into French. As a result the methodology was renamed in order to ensure that the sense of the methodology remained true when translated into French. This suggests a level of understanding and engagement with the thinking behind the methodology which resulted in him not trying to use an exact translation but rather something that captured the intent of the methodology. However, the methodology, and as will be seen the leader approach to engaging with and making sense of it, was not significantly different from leaders in a range of other countries.

The French leader sought to gain some form of commitment compliance by arousing leader curiosity and getting their commitment to engaging in the data gathering stage of the methodology. He was then asked what advice he would give those leader colleagues in the meeting who had not yet engaged with the methodology:

I was asked to give you my advice as leaders:

- You will face some difficulties;
- It's not always an easy journey;
- First, management change – you will move from known world which is command and control management, it's the easiest way to manage, it's like in the army, I've been in the navy I know how it works, it's efficient, but it's not fit for today's customers and employees so you've got to move from command and control to a role for the leader which is here to support and to help. I spend some time in my teams telling them find new ideas, try, experiment, I'm here and I'm just your biggest fan, I'm here to help you, to release barriers and change the environment and system conditions in order to make your work easier;
- The second one is also a difficult one, what I call the control and regulatory functions – risk, audit, compliance, legal. These functions are used to paper, to procedures, written procedures, written decisions and you have to move to a world where the decisions are based on a clever decision from one guy taking information sometimes by phone, not written information so it means changing the way of working for all these control functions. For audit, for risk you have to assess the risk

and monitor it in a different way so it's a really difficult thing and it's really important all the control functions get on board in the system thinking initiatives;

- Then you've got to manage change because at the same time as you are business as usual you also have to run the change initiatives and sometimes there are some conflicts between the two things.

My advice to you heretics - was that the term? (laughter), although it seems a bit pretentious as I've just started a few months ago:

- You will need energy, you will need engagement in order to drive your team in order to lead the change, to engage your colleagues to change the views of all the functions in your business unit;
- You will get tremendous successes – publish them, make lots of noise about them;
- Sometimes you will get to a dead end, when you get to a dead end you just move to another idea.

There are many sensemaking elements in this piece of advice by the leader. Interestingly, in making sense of what it feels like to engage with the methodology the leader is in effect giving the leaders in the meeting a preunderstanding story to help counter modernist preunderstanding of change that they may hold – he is giving them a memory of the future. In his own retrospective sensemaking he is setting the scene to influence the future sensemaking of the leaders he is giving advice to, and he incorporates attributions of responsibility with the words 'engagement' and 'drive' (the leader who is persistent in driving forward the methodology and convincing others to change their mindset) and unity (the collective others such as audit and governance functions that you will have to do battle with). In Chapter 3 I found leaders using these same storytelling tropes and there seems to be an element of passing on of these attributions by leaders.

The language in his story is of a journey, and like any good story it is fraught with risks and challenges. It is a journey from a known world to a new and unknown world. But this journey is not a straightforward move from one to another and he warns that the necessary pragmatic approach of leaders balancing the old world (business as usual) with the new world (new ways of thinking, leading and organizing) will inevitably lead to conflicts. The old world won't give up without a fight. This is a common theme in the sensemaking stories of leaders who have engaged with the methodology.

The language he uses could suggest that the power of modernist preunderstanding to overwhelm a new mindset is evident in his own advice. When he says '*you've got to manage change because at the same time as you are business as usual you also have to run the change initiatives*' it appears he is using a modernist perspective of change as an epi-phenomenon, an initiative, which can or should be managed. However, displacing a concept is not the same as rejecting an old one for a new one, and shared language from an expanded and reconceptualized concept can lead to confusion. I consider that I have a postmodern ontological perspective, but I still have concepts of leading, organizing and change. I also have a concept of change initiatives, albeit very different from the epiphenomenon of a modernist change ontology. As a postmodern leader I don't manage change, but I do manage the process of understanding and navigating the constant stream of flux that is the organizational environment. So my interpretation of his language is that it could be consistent with a developing new concept of leading and change. I say 'developing' because the leader says he just started a few months ago and as was seen in Chapter 3, leaders talked about taking 18 months to two years to really 'get it' in terms of the new mindset. A leader who has engaged with and is embracing the methodology might be expected to still be using some old-world terminology even if the meaning has changed.

The group of leaders then worked through a case study taking them through the application of the methodology in one area of the business:

> Facilitator– let's throw it open for discussion. In the case study we tried to take you through the methodology [change model being used] and particularly going into that data gathering phase where you suddenly start to see a story emerging. In the room I was in there was almost anger – who is responsible for this?, why is this happening?, which is the typical response, there must be people responsible, who can I sack? (laughter). But the real story is that we [the leaders in the case study] had a dashboard of data that showed everything is ok but when you get into the work (you've heard that phrase get into the work a lot today) and see for yourself what's really happening a very different picture emerges.
>
> So how did that feel for you as you went through that process, what were some of the emotions that were going on?

It seems to me that the facilitator is pointing out the cognitive dissonance that leaders will start to experience when they themselves uncover data that conflicts with their current understanding of reality. The facilitator is also highlighting the dissonance reduction and rationalizing behavior that they are initially likely to engage in, i.e. anger and finding someone to blame. If you can't deny the reality you can at least deflect the blame for it on to someone else. The facilitator asked the leaders in the meeting to say how they felt as they viewed the data in the case study:

- Disbelief.
- When you see the opportunity for improvement you feel quite optimistic.

- For me the one thing that struck me was we looked at it through a lens apart from the customer lens. We were looking at it through an efficiency lens, an employee engagement lens, whatever but actually we weren't really thinking about the person who was making the call. We were thinking inwards instead of outwards about the customer which is typical of what we do here.
- And perhaps actually we think upwards rather than inwards, the hierarchy and feeding it rather than how am I serving the customer?
- We've moved to a culture where we want to take reports and we want to use quite simple dashboards and that does make life simpler, but we've also got this view that we want the one version of the truth and those reports [dashboards] were true but they were measuring the wrong thing and actually someone who receives these reports it's important to remember to scrutinize and think from a customer perspective.
- The measures we have in place in the business aren't necessarily telling us what we think they're telling us.
- We were stunned by if you stood back and said if you were looking at this from a compliance standpoint it'd be perfectly acceptable but if you flip the lens and you said from a customer and we look at the customer, like it's not [acceptable]... and then you say to implement this thing you're probably going to have to put some principles that you've agreed to so that we align our functions coz I think there's a natural conflict with governance and compliance here.
- Facilitator: 'I think Governance and Compliance have got a view on that ... [laughter].

The sensemaking is of disbelief and leaders stunned that such a situation as in the case study could arise, although one saw the opportunity that the new information offered. But mostly, the leaders were taken aback and started to interpret what they had seen. The use of the concept of a lens to help this sensemaking suggests that leaders are beginning to understand that there is not, as one leader describes it, one version of the truth. The truth depends on the lens you are using to view the world, and the leaders are beginning to acknowledge that there are many possible lenses, each of which will produce a different version of the truth even when looking at the same data, in much the same way the Actuarial Director in Chapter 4 talked of multiple realities, all of which were correct. None is wrong per se, and the current dashboard is 'true, but they were measuring the wrong thing". So the leader sensemaking is moving to a recognition that there are multiple truths and multiple realities. There is an axiom in organizations that what you measure is what you get. From a postmodern perspective it would be more accurate to say that the lens you use to decide what to measure and then how you interpret what you measured determines the reality you get. The leaders' current lens is an efficiency one but when they looked at the same data through a customer lens they found that not only was performance significantly worse than they thought, so was efficiency. A new lens turned the existing reality of efficiency into a new reality of inefficiency. This acceptance of multiple realities allowed leaders to start thinking about their perspective on organizing – from the current internal perspective of hierarchical and functional structure of organization toward a customer-based process flow approach. More organizing than organization.

Even though some of the leaders had not yet engaged with the methodology, they were beginning to identify with the storytelling trope of attribution of unity that they had heard previously in the session and identified the function of Governance and Compliance as a collective obstacle to any new mindset and that they would have to do battle with. The leader from this area of the business challenged that assumption:

> I need to respond to the challenge on behalf of the audit function. So let me just say I'm a believer now having seen this and so it's more likely that you'll get audit points for NOT doing it [methodology] in future than for doing it (laughter). So we've kind of bought into this and we'll need to have conversations with colleagues in compliance and with the line managers about where the balance of risk and control needs to rest but we're bought into this so that will influence the way we audit processes but we can also apply it [the methodology] to the way in which we conduct audits. My own feeling is there's quite a lot of failure demand on Audit which we'll want to make more transparent and bounce back to the sources of that. I don't want anyone to say that Audit's an excuse for not doing this. Done intelligently there's no reason why you can't get on with this from an Audit perspective.

> It strikes me that .... I accept the customer thing .... But a lot of this stems from a lack of trust in people that those controls are put in place on top of the controls, on top of the controls .... It ultimately boils down that if you don't trust people then ultimately you'll end up with a lot of people covering their backsides so to speak because there must be a culture within Group [senior leadership board of the company] that actually suggests that failure is just not an option, so it doesn't matter how much it costs or what the cost benefits are of doing this, just do it because it doesn't really matter, we're not a profit driven organization, we're a don't screw up organization. And, yeah, I don't think it's just the customer focus, this is a cultural problem that exists in any organization because sometimes you just work on the basis of it looks great and I don't need to look at it, and it's inefficient and people need to be tasked with fixing their problems.

The leader of the Audit and Governance function, which the previous speaker had declared an obstacle to mindset change, starts by making it clear that he is a 'believer' and jokes that far from being an obstacle, he is going to challenge leaders who don't embrace the methodology. He then says what he thinks that the problem is with the current leadership mindset. There is a lack of trust permeating the organization and it comes from a fear of failure at the very top of the organization. He seems to surface an unsayable when he challenges the espoused theory in action that this is a profit-driven organization and says it is really a 'don't screw up' organization. He is suggesting that current Group [senior leader] theories-in-use are undermining the espoused theory in action (Argyris, 1990). In my notes of the meeting I recorded my thoughts:

> ... well that was quite an elephant in the room being put firmly center stage! Interesting that there was no noticeable discomfort, looks or fidgeting by the Group leaders in the room. In fact they were nodding their heads.

My sense was that this was a leader who had close contact with senior leaders as part of his role and that there had been enough of a shift in mindset at senior leadership level for this leader to be able to speak so openly and say what previously would have probably remain unsaid.

The leader is also saying to those leaders about to engage with the methodology, don't start writing your sensemaking story of a collective audit and governance entity that needs overcome in battle quite yet – we've bought into the methodology. My first reflection after the meeting was that he was saying save your story trope of attribution of unity for those functions who actually deserve it. But on further reflection I thought he was saying, although perhaps not in exactly the way I am interpreting, beware the trap of attributing unity in your stories. Like the audit function, you might find your attributions are wrong. If the lens we use in our current mindset gives us a partial or even flawed reality, the lens we use in our sensemaking story of engaging with the postmodern methodology can result in an equally partial or flawed reality. For me as both a researcher and a practitioner this seems like a profound learning. There does seem a strong theme in post-engagement leader stories of having a *better* understanding of reality than the modernist leaders we have left behind. The real lesson is that we have a *different* understanding of reality and the reason the methodology stresses the constant cycle of critical reflexivity is a recognition that failure to do this will lead to a modernist thinking trap of change having been 'done' and that our new better reality should be embedded in the organization. But if postmodern leaders accept that there is no single truth and that our current reality at any given time is only one partial version of reality, we must keep challenging that reality. This insight is of course my personal sensemaking after reflection on the meeting transcript. As an observer I cannot know without having discussed it with those present the extent to which it was shared by anyone else. I have, however, used it as discussion point with leaders since this time and built it in to my preunderstanding stories that I give to leaders when seeking their initial commitment compliance.

Ah-ha! moments were also an important aspect of this collective post-engagement sensemaking:

> Sometimes when you're looking at this stuff in detail suddenly a light bulb moment goes on for you as a leader and you say 'actually some of this rubbish that we're seeing is something that I've directly or indirectly created by a decision I've taken or an instruction I've given. Has that lightbulb moment gone on for anyone here? Something you've done that's led to this type of Frankenstein's monster.

In Chapter 3 leaders talked about specific moments in time when they suddenly had a realization that their thinking was flawed and that they needed to change. They used various terms to describe these moments: ah-ha!, insight, road to Damascus experience, epiphany, tipping point, bolt out the blue and Whoa! moments. Now the facilitator was talking about light bulb moments. For consistency, I have used the term ah-ha! moments to cover all these terms used by leaders.

The leaders volunteered their ah-ha! moments:

Speaker 3: very quickly, my lightbulb moment or as [name] eloquently put it, my oh fuck moment, was the epiphany event that we were actually all together [lists the senior leaders that were present] and we looked at the data we'd gathered. And I used to walk into the contact center and celebrate with everyone who hit their sales conversion target, had beaten it and absolutely applaud them because that was the metric that was most important to us, it was the be all and end all of sales effectively. And there were 600 people doing this on a daily basis ... and we thought that was all fine.

But the data we were finding and that I didn't want to hear was that I'd incentivized people.. and the incentives were up to 30%, you could earn 30% by meeting the target [for converting calls into sales]. And we did an analysis of the people who had the highest conversion rate. They were the same people that when they'd got to their conversion rate in their day, they chose to take their allotted time off [time allowed off the phones]. Now you're probably .... Well you are ... looking at me going why are we still employing that muppet, this was a guy running a huge number of people in operations but I take it you've had ... we've all had ... that epiphany moment. The very people who I thought were the best were actually doing things adverse to delivering a great customer experience, coz when the phones were getting really hot and people [customers] were just about to leave work or were just getting home from work, they [the staff] weren't making themselves available coz their purpose was about THEIR conversion rate and not about serving the customers. And it's a simple example like that makes you think 'I need to get into the work in a much different way'.

Speaker 3 is clear that the data he had gathered when doing action learning research on his own department created an ah-ha! moment that prevented him from being able to rationalize what he was learning. He had uncovered a leadership heresy – his deeply held belief that a conversion target for staff improved performance but that actually made performance worse. This seems to be another example of the unsayable being said. Frontline staff and managers will have been aware of the game-playing by apparently high-performing staff, but it would not be acknowledged or surfaced. The staff engaging in the game playing would not point out that they were cheating the system and frontline managers were praised for managing performance and so would be unlikely to point out that it was illusory. However, the data gathered using the methodology carried sufficient credibility for the leader to positively respond to his own revealing of this heresy. By presenting this example of the importance of surfacing the unsayable, the leader is also telling the leaders present at the meeting that this is something they must be prepared for. He is creating some preunderstanding or memory of the future about how challenging the methodology will be for them and that they must expect to embrace similar heresies.

Other leaders who had engaged with the methodology told similar stories:

Speaker 4: and what's interesting about that is actually the staff weren't trying to earn a 30% bonus, they were trying to avoid a bollocking from their manager. The fear of the stick was a much greater motivator for these people than the lure of the carrot. There was (sic) people being marched out the building because they hadn't hit their conversion target for that month. Now where you find a target in an operation there will be a cheat and leaders will cheat to make sure they hit their targets .... Now I know this is shocking, but you know what? The mea culpa moment was realizing we're all responsible for creating this system.

Speaker 4 worked in the same business area as speaker 3, and both leaders seemed comfortable now saying what would have been unsayable before engaging with the methodology. The leaders admit that they had created a culture of fear and that their thinking was driving the wrong behavior by staff. Clearly there has been a change in mindset that allowed the leaders to reveal these unsayables and embrace what would have been heresy before, i.e. that targets and incentives will always drive the wrong behaviors. It seems to me that the leader talk of ah-ha! moments confirms my sense that the retrospective creation of these allows them to make a sensible story in which they used to be 'old world' but saw the light and now have knowledge which gives them a new world of reality. In addition, speaker 2's statement that his 'mea culpa moment was realizing that we're all part of that system' is a recognition of the methodology concept of 'leader thinking results in the system, which in turn results in organizational performance'. Leaders are not separate from the system or the performance of staff, their thinking is directly responsible for it. While this might not be a problem if staff and the system appear to be performing well, taking responsibility for it when both are shown to be performing poorly is more difficult for leaders. In this case the leaders were clearly accepting full responsibility for, and without rationalizing, the data showing poor performance.

Another leader then gave an example of her ah-ha! moment:

Speaker 5: Our facilitator [in the case study exercise] was trying to take us through the data and she was slowly giving us more and more information as we went, but literally every time we got one more piece of information we'd try and solve – 'why aren't we doing this? Have you thought about this? Why don't we do that? And I had this epiphany moment and said how many times do I try to solve before my folks have even really told me the story and what the problem is? Maybe they've done it and I haven't really listened to it because I was so quick to get the answer because we've got to keep going or because I'd seen it before and we extrapolate out or we make these assumptions and we've seen it before so actually we know that solution … and we jump. As leader that was a bit of a …. Oooph… I've gotta stop thinking like that.

This short description is of an ah-ha! moment that happened just 30 minutes previously. The leader had been part of a small group being led through presentation of a case study of data gathering using the methodology and her description of what happened contains important elements of sensemaking. My own sense initially as she described what was happening was that she was describing an interesting observation rather than an ah-ha! moment but then as she questioned her long held practice of jumping to solutions it did seem to me that there was a questioning of her current way of thinking. There was also a recognition of the impact of preunderstanding on her leadership thinking. If she's seen something similar before, she jumps to solutions based on what she's done in similar situations before. The leader seemed to suggest that her current mindset was the 'if it looks like a duck and quacks like a duck, it's a duck' practice commonly quoted in organizations, but her epiphany was that this was not always the right thing to do and that in future she would challenge herself before moving to solutions. My own sensemaking of this was that it was unlikely her behavior would change so radically based on the insight from just this one event. I recalled the leaders in Chapter 3 who talked about their ah-ha! moments at presentations but who then conceded that it actually took them up to a year to actually 'get it' in terms of mindset change. However, in this leader's case I felt that she had certainly had a curiosity engendering ah-ha! moment, and this would create helpful new preunderstanding prior to her engagement with the methodology.

The meeting finished with the facilitator asking leaders who had previously engaged with the methodology to sum it up in one word. The leaders' responses were:

- Eye opening
- Energizing
- Insightful
- Common sense
- Liberating
- Game-changing
- Obvious
- Addictive
- Works

This was an opportunity for leaders to establish some further preunderstanding with those leaders yet to engage with the methodology. Their choice of words suggests some positive experiences can be expected. The two word 'eye opening' carries connotation of a new perspective and connects with other leaders talk about a different lens to view reality. 'Insightful' links to the ah-ha! moments discussed earlier in the meeting and 'liberating' suggests a freedom from the constraints of our current mindset. 'Energizing', 'works', 'game changing' and 'addictive' imply that engaging with the methodology is a positive experience for leaders that they will sustain over the long term.

The words that might seem less obvious, even contradictory given the radical change of thinking that the leaders had just described, are 'obvious' and 'common sense'. On first reflection these words reminded me of the reactions of leaders to the war room data in Chapter 8. When confronted with the data that showed the impact of their thinking, they said there was nothing new and that they didn't already know. If the methodology was obvious and just common sense it might suggest that it is something leaders already know and nothing particularly new. After all, are there any leaders who would say that they lack common sense or can't spot the obvious? However, after further reflection and interpretation of what the leaders were saying, I put their words into the wider context of what they had been describing over the previous two hours and my sense of their meaning is that far from being a rationalizing of threatening evidence such as the leaders in the war room engaged in, this was a profound statement of the change in their mindset. The methodology had presented them with challenges to their existing mindsets and shown that they had been responsible for the poor performance, culture of fear and cheating that they had shared with the rest of the group. They had engaged over a period of months and years with the methodology, and as can be seen from their contributions they were now firm advocates of it. It is a measure of the adoption of a new mindset that it is no longer challenging but rather now so embedded and obvious that it is just common sense.

Conclusion

The leaders told exciting and plausible stories and the general thrust was as my research notes captured over the time I worked with them. However, the stories were typical of most leader sensemaking I observed in that they omitted some of what happened (mostly when things went 'wrong'), rearranged history so that events appeared more linear and sequential than they were (such as the descriptions when, or indeed even if, they experienced ah-ha! moments) and embellished events using story telling tropes to make them more exciting (particularly the role of the individual leader as the hero, whereas my research often found the leader lagging behind others in terms of 'getting it'). What I believe I witnessed in this meeting was the selective use of events to construct stories and embellishment to make the story more interesting which moves the leader from wrestling with their own sensemaking to a position where they are becoming the sensegivers of the methodology to others. History belongs to those who write it and the social nature of sensemaking demonstrated in this meeting illustrates that our sensemaking 'history' is a social construct, a fable agreed upon. But fable or not, it is the agreed history and the agreed truth, until such times as a heretic challenges the new orthodoxy.

The potential problem created by this retrospective sensemaking of engaging with, interpreting and making sense of a complex and messy process of mindset change is that it may create a false preunderstanding for others about what to expect when they initially engage with the methodology, at which stage it will seem anything but obvious or common sense. The second potential problem is that it can become self-fulfilling in that leaders have been given a memory of the future which they will then use to construct their own sensemaking story – surely I too shall have to battle courageously against the forces of opposition, presumably I too shall have my ah-ha! moment, and so forth.

References

Argyris, C. 1990. *Overcoming Organizational Defenses: Facilitating Organizational Learning*, Boston, Allyn and Bacon.

Argyris, C. 2004. *Reasons and Rationalizations: The Limits to Organizational Knowledge*, Oxford, Oxford University Press.

Part IV

Conclusion – Influencing Sensemaking

14 Sensemaking

Recipes, Plate Spinning or Web Weaving?

Two things strike me about the post-engagement sensemaking stories of leaders in the last Chapter. The first is how similar they are to the leader's stories in Chapter 3. The second is how different they are to my observations of the sensemaking I observed with this same group of leaders in the years prior to this collective sensemaking session.

If I had interviewed myself in Chapter 3 my sensemaking story would have followed the same pattern as the other leaders. It would have started with my setting out of my preunderstanding and experience setting me firmly in the modernist old world. This was followed by my own ah-ha! moment. I had just finished reading Beauvois and Joule's (1996) radical theory of cognitive dissonance and I had a moment of insight that linked my understanding of cognitive dissonance and the transformation methodology I was engaging with. At that moment I realized that my current thinking about leadership and organization was flawed. I too then became the lonely champion of change and fought for a year to be gain leader commitment compliance in my own organization. After heroic persistence on my part I convinced the Chief Executive to support the use of the methodology in a business area that was experiencing severe performance issues. I worked with leaders who didn't 'get it' but won them over to a radical new way of thinking and the end result was a transformation of that area of the business and a new leadership culture. Having moved to a new mindset I too believed that I could never go back to my old way of thinking and I questioned every aspect of experience in life from my new postmodern perspective.

However, following my years of research and after understanding the impact of the nine sensemaking elements I observed, I have reinterpreted my past experiences and reconstructed my story. My reconstruction looks like this:

- I still explain my preunderstanding and experience prior to engaging with the various methodologies I have used as these are important to my thinking at that time. However I was not a committed modernist one day and a postmodern thinker the next. For a start, the development of my postmodern thinking started long before I engaged with the methodology or started my research – I had been interested in the writing of Heraclitus for some time before this although I struggled to relate his work to organizational theory. Secondly, as I explored in Chapter 11, my sensemaking now embraces the compresence of opposites and I am comfortable with being a postmodern modernist (or should that be modernist postmodernist?)

- My story still has an ah-ha! moment, but I now acknowledge that I only recognized it as such some time afterwards when a number of things came together unexpectedly and without even realizing I had been pondering them and all of a sudden I got 'a sense of connection for which the only meaningful response seems to be Whoa!' (Bellinger, 2017). I do still believe that Beauvois and Joule's work was a defining moment in my sensemaking of sensemaking, but I only came to realize it 18 months after I had first read their book and after I had revisited it several times. I had a sense it was important to my understanding of sensemaking, but it took time to realize just how important it was. My first sensemaking story followed the pattern of leaders I had observed in my research in that it placed my ah-ha! moment much earlier in the timeline than it actually occurred, because it does make a much better and plausible story.
- It is accurate to say I was a lonely advocate of the methodology but on reflection it was not my heroic championing of it that convinced the Chief Executive to commit to it. Yes, I had recommended it to him a number of times, but it was sheer desperation on his part that led him to agree to try the methodology. He had tried numerous modernist change methodologies but none had resolved the problems with this area of this business. It was only when he had exhausted modernist methodologies and was exasperated that he eventually said something along the lines of 'ok Ron you've been banging on about this methodology for a while so I'll give you a chance to prove it works'. Of course recognizing that the Chief Executive only gave me a chance because he felt he had no other option does not quite have the same storytelling impact as my heroic conversion of his thinking.
- Yes, I did work with leaders who didn't 'get it' and won them over to a radical new way of thinking and the end result was a transformation of that area of the business and a new leadership culture.
- I used to believe that I could never go back to my old way of thinking, but my research has led me to a better understanding of a postmodernist (or my version of it anyway) understanding of sensemaking that can embrace multiple realities and paradigms. I reject the story telling attribute of unity in which I have knowledge of reality and those who do not share my interpretation are the collective ignorant others.

As I reflected on my two sensemaking stories I was reminded of Walter Scott's tale of Marmion:

> 'Oh! What a tangled web we weave when first we practice to deceive'
>
> (Scott, 1808).

In Chapter 13 I said that the sensemaking stories of the leaders did not quite match my observations of how they seemed to be making sense of the interventions as they engaged with the methodology. There was an element of creating a good story, a fable agreed upon. Now I have just told you that my own original sensemaking story, which matched those of the leaders in Chapters 3 and 13, had to be reinterpreted once I had reflected on my research. Am I suggesting that all sensemaking is some form of deception – of self and others? The answer contains a compresence of opposites – yes *and* no.

First the 'yes'. My research has demonstrated that leader sensemaking is not a rational and empirical process that drives us, like some sort of laboratory scientist or Sherlock Homes, to create an objective reality. It is a process of us rationalizing what we are experiencing in a way that makes a good and plausible story for us. As we have seen, that rationalizing, interpretation and story construction is heavily influenced by existing ontology, orthodoxy, pre-understanding, cognitive dissonance, and defensive reasoning. The reality we construct is shaped by these sensemaking elements and can only ever be one interpretation from countless possible interpretations. We have also seen how the desire to construct a good story leads to us adopting storytelling tropes which embellish the story and make it more interesting. We all want to be the heroes in our stories, even as when as in the war room example we had failed and so we used the storytelling tropes of attribution of responsibility (us as heroes valiantly battling resistance), and unity (stereotyping the other leaders as an undifferentiated entity of others). I did not capture the sensemaking stories of the leaders who had chosen not to engage after the war room, but I can be fairly confident that they did not paint themselves as villains of their own stories, and they would almost certainly have contained similar storytelling attributes, possibly telling of their heroic struggle to defend the organization from a damaging methodology being promoted by zealots who were out of touch with reality. The end result is at least two versions of reality – each equally valid but deceptive in that we have filtered our interpretations to deliver our good story.

A common example of our sensemaking deception is the frequent talk of ah-ha! moments by leaders, me included. I am not suggesting that there are no contemporaneous ah-ha! moments, but they are much rarer than the leader stories would have you believe. When pressed to reflect on their ah-ha! moments most leaders tended to acknowledge that the ah-ha! happened after a period of reflection but their stories place them earlier as this makes the story more plausible and sensible.

Despite being 'yes', the answer is also no, sensemaking is not about deceiving of self or others. Deception is trying to get someone to accept as true something which is not. Sensemaking is about trying to establish what the truth of our experiences is. It may be only a partial and selective recollection, and it may not be a totally reliable interpretation, but it is our best attempt, and it is our reality unless or until further sensemaking or reflection leads us to reinterpret as has happened with my own sensemaking story. For example, the leaders ah-ha! moments did happen and they are real. In each case the leaders identified what they considered to be seminal moments in their sensemaking, and it makes perfect sense to position the ah-ha! at that seminal moment, even if we only recognized it as such sometime later.

Are storytelling tropes not by definition deceptive? No, they may lead to us embellishing our sensemaking stories, but they are not the villains of sensemaking. They are linguistic metaphors that make our stories more sensible, interesting and therefore effective. We simply have to remember that our, or anyone else's, sensemaking story is an *interpretation* constructed to help us make sense of things, to justify our actions and to shape future actions, but as a result we do need to treat them with a little caution and not as if they are scientific papers subject to tests of validity and reliability.

Ultimately, questions of whether sensemaking is true/false or right/wrong are based on the wrong premise. Sensemaking is not right or wrong, true or deceptive. It is about an endless construction of our reality and in an organizational setting that reality is a co-constructed social reality not an objective reality. A much more important question which I hope my research has gone some way to address is how an understanding of sensemaking can help leaders and interventionists in organizations challenge current orthodoxies.

Conclusion

If you jumped to this final chapter hoping to skip the detail and, as you would in most modernist writings on change, find a recipe for managing your own or someone else's sensemaking then you will be disappointed. Sensemaking and change share a common thread – they emerge from the continuous flux of organizational life and that flux cannot, with any certainty or predictability, be forecast or controlled. However, I am not proposing a nihilistic perspective, and I hope that my research has demonstrated that sensemaking, as it is happening, can be understood, responded to, influenced and navigated. To return to the cooking metaphor, we have the ingredients, but we need to create our recipe depending on the circumstances, and it will need constant modification as we find more or less ingredients are needed.

But enough of the cooking metaphor. I think it should by now be clear that helping leaders to make sense of challenges to their current thinking is a fine balancing act of constant awareness of, and response to, the nine elements of sensemaking, each of which can help or hinder the process (often both at the same time). I did for a time use a plate spinning metaphor since it seemed to me that an interventionist needs to be constantly aware of all nine elements but cannot be attending to all at once. And so like the circus plate spinning act, the interventionist must run from plate to plate re-energizing their spinning but watching to see which other plate is nearest to falling off its pole next. The only problem with this metaphor is that it treats each sensemaking element as something distinct from the others and that operates independently.

The fact is that all sensemaking elements are interconnected and influence all the others. To further complicate matters, sensemaking is a largely social activity conducted with others. Finally, sensemaking is an ongoing activity and no interventionist, even an active participant such as I was, will be present at all times. The nine elements of sensemaking can become active at any stage and when they do they have an influence on, or can trigger, any of the other sensemaking elements and so the metaphor that works best in my story of sensemaking is a spiders web. Each element is intertwined with each of the eight other elements and when one is affected the others may be activated in response, or not. And when we factor in that each sensemaking element can have both a positive and negative impact on leader acceptance of challenge to their existing thinking there is a possible permutation of effects many times greater than any interventionist's capacity to even identify, far less manage.

A question I have not specifically addressed up to this point is whether my research only applies to leader sensemaking of postmodern change methodologies. The answer is no. I was researching leader sensemaking as they made decisions about whether or not to engage with the methodologies I was using, not their sensemaking of any given methodology. While my own postmodern ontology has driven my sensemaking story of my research I believe that the elements of sensemaking are universal and will apply in any organizational setting where a leader or interventionist is seeking to challenge current ontologies, orthodoxies, paradigms or mindsets.

Finally, how do I know that there are only nine sensemaking elements and not ten, elven or more? The answer is I don't. I have presented the elements I observed over a period of ten years working with leaders across the globe and I do not claim them to be a definitive list. Please note that I used the word 'observed' not 'identified'. If my research has any value to interventionists it is that I have synthesized and pragmatized existing research on individual elements of sensemaking in a way that interventionists might find useful. The outcome of my research may not be a recipe, but I hope it is a useful handbook for heretics.

References

Beauvois, J.-L. & Joule, R.-V. 1996. *A Radical Dissonance Theory*, London, Taylor and Francis.

Bellinger, G. 2017. Really? Whoa!. https://www.linkedin.com/pulse/really-whoa-gene-bellinger [Online]. [Accessed 17th Feb 2017].

Scott, W. 1808. *Marmion; A Tale of Flodden Field*, Edinburgh, Archibald Constable and Company.

Index

For Product Safety Concerns and Information please contact our EU representative GPSR@taylorandfrancis.com
Taylor & Francis Verlag GmbH, Kaufingerstraße 24, 80331 München, Germany

www.ingramcontent.com/pod-product-compliance
Ingram Content Group UK Ltd.
Pitfield, Milton Keynes, MK11 3LW, UK
UKHW022355190926
475702UK00015B/2300
9781032014753